Teaching English in Church

A "How-to" Guide

William Bradridge

CONTENTS

ACKNOWLEDGMENTS

Thank you and acknowledgements to:

Louisa Walsh, Course Director, Christian TEFL
James Myles WPCA Church, Belfast
Carys Woodbridge ELT Baptist Church. London
Sue Wood, Belmont Church, Exeter
Ferris Lindsey, London
Kathy Baxter, London
Kerry McEwan, Kent
Sophie Gower, Exeter
two:nineteen: organisers of the English
Teaching and Outreach Forum, enabling
networking amongst Christian ESL teachers, a
sharing of ideas and best ELT practices. This
forum was invaluable in the writing of this guide.

To all those who contributed with comments and
suggestions anonymously.

CHAPTER 1

INTRODUCTION TO TEACHING ENGLISH IN CHURCH

Background to Teaching English in Church

Since launching Christian TEFL in 2011, we have had the immense privilege of attending many Christian shows, conferences, seminars, and talks. Our primary aim is to reach people who are keen on training to teach English and then serve overseas in mission.

However, one unexpected (but equally pleasurable) outcome of these meetings and discussions has been speaking to Christians eager to talk to us for a different reason: they have wanted to see how they might use their English to reach people for the gospel, not overseas, but right where they are, through their local church.

This has been incredibly heartening and humbling. God has clearly called some Christians to respond to a real need in their communities. The question for them has often been: *"What now?"* and *"Where do I start?"*

The Christians we have spoken to have had a variety of aims. Some were keen to start an initiative at their church and wanted to know where to begin organisationally. Others were looking to join an existing church English teaching programme but wanted some signposting and a flavour of what it was likely to look like.

We have been able to speak to both sets of people – but have had nothing for them to take away in their hands that would serve as both a practical start-up guide for potential organisers and a *"What does teaching in church involve?"* brief for volunteers.

As a result, the seeds for this guide were sown through engagement with Christians wishing to share the gospel right where they are. Since then, we've done a lot more research and connected with organisations and Christians involved in the front line of this great ministry. We can now offer you a picture of the challenges, best practice, top tips, and useful resources that they have kindly shared with us.

My grateful thanks to all who have contributed to the creation of this guide. May God bless, protect, and encourage you in your work.

William Bradridge
Christian TEFL
September 2017

Who is this guide for?

This short publication is designed as a **next step guide** for any Christian thinking about serving in their local communities through teaching English.

It is intended to be an easy-to-read-and-digest introduction. We presume that you will have little or no teaching experience and so have aimed to make this guide as practical as possible for the new teacher. However, if you do have teaching experience, we hope you will find the first-hand accounts from Christians teaching in this way and links to further resources equally useful.

We believe that this will be of use to you in any English-speaking country, although many of the examples and experiences do come from the UK.

We hope that this will be of help if you are one of or all of the following:

...a potential organiser of a church programme looking to teach English; you will find ideas here on considerations for setting up, recruiting volunteers and publicising your programme locally.

...a volunteer who wishes to join an existing programme; you can skip the organisational elements and jump straight to what to teach (found in Chapter 3), ideas for how to teach, organising classes and the roles of volunteers, along with a useful index of teaching resources.

At the end of some chapters, you will find a page of further resources, where you can take your interest in any particular area we have covered a little further.

Our hope is that you will find this a useful and encouraging springboard to getting involved. Also, that in time you might wish to share your experiences with us so we can help inspire Christians to this ministry in the future.

CHAPTER 2

WHY REACH PEOPLE BY
TEACHING ENGLISH?

If you are a Christian reading this, then you are probably aware of a couple of verses from the Bible which speak of the great commission to go and tell the world about Jesus:

"Therefore go and make disciples of all nations, baptising them in the name of the Father and of the Son and of the Holy Spirit." Matthew 28:19

"And he said to them, "Go into all the world and proclaim the gospel to the whole creation." Mark 16:15

Famous church leaders and preachers have taken up this call. As Spurgeon said:

"It is the whole business of the whole church to preach the whole gospel to the whole world."

So for Christians, the biblical mandate is clear, although many of us may not see ourselves in the 'traditional' missionary mould. Possibly going overseas to spread the gospel is simply not on our horizon.

However, a very exciting development is unfolding

right where we are. The fact is that, in most English-speaking countries, there is a steady influx of migrants arriving to live, work or study. In the UK, for example, net migration has been on the rise since the 1980s and has increased dramatically since 2000. In the year to September 2014, net migration into the UK was **298,000, according to the UK Office for National Statistics**.

As Christians, we may not need statistics to tell us things have changed. The very reason you are reading this document could simply be that you are looking for a meaningful response to the increase in different languages you hear around you.

While our responses to these changes may be varied, we can't ignore the obvious. Many people from overseas, who find themselves living in an English-speaking country, need to learn or improve their English. They also may not have heard the gospel.

That means there are plenty of opportunities for Christians to help meet both of these needs.

So, a knowledge of English in itself is a vital tool for integration into the UK or another-English-speaking country, but it could also be so much more. Just think, through the link provided by English classes, your church could also be:

...a welcoming, safe place, especially where someone has known fear and persecution at home.

...a family and community to people when their home is far away.

...the place where migrants to English-speaking countries learn about Jesus and come to a saving knowledge of His love and sacrifice.

N.B. For ease of reference, **migrants to English-speaking countries** will be referred to as **internationals** in this guide or, when talking about English classes, as **learners**.

Timing is crucial

It's an obvious statement to make but in English-speaking countries, a working knowledge of the indigenous language is vital for integration and a harmonious society.

People from overseas who are living in English-speaking countries and who have enough English to communicate, and are able to work or study, are likely to be happier, more connected, productive, and contribute positively to life there. When internationals want to communicate with their neighbours and are able to do so, it breaks down barriers and helps alleviate suspicion and mistrust between individuals and communities.

However, time is ticking in terms of reaching many internationals. As the Christian organisation, two:nineteen (supporting English teaching in churches) points out, there may be a critical window of opportunity after which an international may stop looking outward, become less interested in learning English, and retreat inwards. The ability to reach individuals for Christ through teaching English locally appears time-critical.

"...the first six months after their arrival in a country is the critical period in determining how well the integration process goes, if at all." two:nineteen (part of Serving in Mission)

So, there is an urgency to the work of reaching internationals. But let us also not forget that whenever anyone steps out in faith for Christ to do something for their neighbour, the blessings are rarely channelled one way.

What is also clear is that cross-cultural influences on our own churches can be invigorating; helping prevent us from getting stuck in our ways and encouraging us, as a church, to examine **why we do what we do**.

Kathy Baxter, who has plenty of experience teaching English in church, says that she has learned a great deal through the hospitality, generosity, and gratitude of the internationals she has met. She writes;

"It's incredibly humbling when a refugee family, living on benefits, provides you with a wonderful meal simply to say thank you for teaching them.

Many cultures have a very generous view of hospitality and welcome that puts my Western life in perspective. In addition, our lives are enriched and challenged in positive ways when our own assumptions about other cultures are confronted. We are changed by the experience, as much as our learners are enriched by improved English skills."

Embarking on such adventures is likely to involve challenges as well as unexpected joys. So we can expect to learn and grow as we serve. We have so much to learn as well as impart!

Where do internationals come from?

There are various reasons why people from overseas may be living in an English-speaking country. We have detailed some of these reasons below, although it isn't an extensive list. They may typically be:

...asylum seekers who may be waiting to find out the status of their leave to remain. They are usually not allowed to work, might be under some emotional and financial stress, on top of any trauma they've experienced in their journey to get here.

...refugees, who have been granted leave to remain in the UK and often have the right to work. They will usually be motivated to learn English and find employment as soon as possible so they can build a life for themselves here. They also might have experienced trauma or loss.

…those rescued from human trafficking. A church in Darlington is working with the rescued, for example, running English conversational classes. The organisation, Hope for Justice, has been instrumental in rescue.

…trailing spouses - a husband or wife who follows their spouse to an English-speaking country for a duration. Often the working partner has an instant community and is practising English by using it every day. This can leave the trailing spouse isolated during the day, especially if their English is poor.

…international students – university towns in English-speaking countries often have a thriving international base. Mostly, students will need to have a high level of English to enter university (often measured by the IELTS exam) and may also be attending a university-led English programme, which focuses on English for academic purposes. However, many will be keen to make connections outside the international student scene and build confidence in conversational English.

…people working in an English-speaking country (sometimes referred to as economic migrants). In the UK at the time of writing, those within the EU have the right to relocate to other member states. As a result, there has been a great influx from Eastern Europe, Spain, and Portugal.

You may have seen a growth of internationals as members of the congregation where you worship and this is often the catalyst for ESL provision by the church. For example, in recent years in the UK, we have seen a growth in church attendees from mainly Catholic traditions from Spain, Greece, and Eastern Europe. Possibly your church has noticed the need for English but hasn't been able to engage with it yet? Well, help is at hand. Let's look at some of the different ways in which we can serve.

How to serve – your choices

"There was an increase in the ethnic minority population in the area. Many were isolated in their homes because they could not speak the language and were therefore afraid to go out. In order to help them to integrate…the church decided to invite them along to English classes…" James Myles, WPCA, Belfast

If you have identified a need for English within your own locality and God is moving you to action, what next? Well, you might choose from one of these four options:

…join an existing teaching English programme. See what is already in place in your local area through churches and other voluntary organisations to see if you can get involved - rather than duplicate effort. Type "**free English classes in xxxxx (your**

location)" in a search engine as a start.

…get help setting up an English teaching programme in your church from established organisations who have done it before. In Reading, UK, the two:nineteen organisation has a model for an English language school (called Bridges) that any church can replicate. At the time of writing, they have helped establish three Bridges-type schools with more to come. From setup documents through to more hands-on consultations, this could be a good place to start. See the resources chapter at the end of this guide for more details.

…start your own English teaching project through your church in response to the need you see around you. This guide is designed to help you get started. Although we hope that if you choose to serve in one of the other ways, you will also find parts of this guide helpful.

…start informal English conversation classes as a 'toe in the water' before considering setting up something more formal with English teaching etc.

All of the above could enable the gospel to spread through our local communities.

In our next chapter, let's move on to explore how the third option (above) might work in practice.

CHAPTER 3

GETTING STARTED

So we have identified that there is a need around us and that we'd like to do something about it. In this chapter, we will look at how we can reach internationals, the type of publicity that can be effective, and how we can recruit helpers and volunteers.

But before we think about reaching the people we'd like to teach, let's start with the need to engage with our church to bless this outreach project.

Church Support

Engaging with and receiving the blessing of your local church for the project ahead is essential to long-term project success. So this should be a priority from the outset.

If your church leaders are behind you, then it is more likely that you will receive the blessing and support of your congregation, too. This blessing may be financial, practical or through prayer. Ultimately, a programme prayed for and supported by the congregation as a whole has more chance of longevity.

Getting the blessing of a church is more than the church donating a room in the building from which to conduct classes. So, talk to your church leader about your vision for the project and speak in terms of outreach. Encourage them to take it as seriously as any other outreach/mission activity and ask for their advice on how best to get the whole church behind the project.

In practical terms, this might involve the occasional slot in the morning service and a regular space in the notice sheets for updates and prayer requests. It may even include funds to purchase essential material and resources. It may involve encouraging the congregation to get alongside learners in a number of ways to show hospitality and a strong welcome. Agree to report back to the leadership or outreach team regularly, invite them to sit in on the occasional lesson and, once the programme is underway, invite the congregation to visit, too.

Do ask about health and safety policies, fire regulations, how and where personal information on volunteers and learners should be kept and stored for reasons of data protection. Also, check that the current insurance policy will cover your programme. If possible, ask someone responsible for these policies to run a brief training session for you and your volunteers.

Working hand in hand with your church is crucial to success. If you can get off on the right foot, then everything else will flow much more easily.

But how do we reach out to find and engage potential English learners? Let's think about this next.

Reaching internationals

Ok, so let's assume that after much prayer and with the blessing of your church, you have decided to start an English teaching programme from scratch.

In addition to the classes themselves, there are a few extras to consider that can make all the difference in terms of attracting people and keeping them coming. We don't want to overwhelm you with extras, but even if you are only in a position to offer no.1 and commit to working towards no.4, that's fine and worth doing. Here is our short list of extras that will help to encourage people to come.

Refreshments
Tea/coffee and a friendly welcome. Remember that your potential learners aren't just accessing a service – they want to connect personally. It may have taken someone with little English and who feels socially isolated a lot of courage to attend. So making time at the beginning for people to come, have a coffee, and chat with other members is warm, welcoming, sets the tone, and helps people feel more at ease.

Crèche
Teaching English classes offered in the daytime will

have a better take-up if a crèche can be offered. Note your church's policy on crèche leaders – a DBS (Disclosure and Barring Service) check may be required for volunteers looking after young children, so check with your church leader or administrator about getting the appropriately qualified people to assist here.

Classes to suit your community or unreached groups

International students, asylum seekers, and those seeking active employment will likely require a different focus in lessons. It would be a good idea to try to get a picture of the main international communities in your local area so you can publicise classes that will most likely meet their needs.

Of course, this may evolve over time when you see who starts coming to class and what their needs are. There is more on tailoring classes around particular needs later on in this guide.

Being good at what you do

It probably goes without saying, but we need to be good at what we do. So if you are teaching, making sure that you have a basic idea of how to structure and plan a lesson to both inform and educate will be vital if your learners are going to be able to improve their English (and, hence, come back for more classes).

Therefore, it is important to have a TEFL or TESOL

qualification. There are many TEFL course options, including online courses, face-to-face courses, and weekend tasters. There is more information on some possibilities on the further research page at the end of this chapter.

Teacher training courses, networking, support, and forums
Having a TEFL/TESOL qualification will help you become more confident as you step into teaching or assisting. You will find some links to TEFL courses for Christians at the end of this chapter. But equally important are being receptive, professional, providing imaginative classes, and having a genuine interest in the people you teach. These should prove a captivating combination.

Learners will come back and word will spread
So, we have looked at what to offer to encourage people to come along and we have outlined some of the additional services you might want to consider offering that will help attract people and make them feel welcome. But how do we reach them to let them know about the programme? We will need to do a little publicity. So let's examine what that might look like next.

Publicity
Now, you will want to get the word out, especially if your target group does not already attend your church regularly, if at all.

While many of the group organisers we asked said that word of mouth was the key way to attract students, to get things started you will certainly need to publicise your efforts to let potential learners know about the programme.

The following is a fairly lengthy list of different ways of doing this. Pick and choose what works best for you and don't feel overwhelmed by the variety of ideas below. Simply select based on your time and resources. Also, you could focus on the ones that you feel would yield the best results locally, prioritising and ticking them off as you do them over time.

Here are some ideas on how you can raise awareness of your new project:

...print some simple flyers to leave at church so people can take them to give to friends.

...tell members of other churches you know in your area. Ask them to put up posters and ask for any volunteers at the same time.

...leaflet local schools, children's centres, libraries, GP surgeries, walk-in centres, and job centres, or call to tell them about the classes and offer to email a flyer they can print off and display.

...tell the local council what you are doing so they can direct enquirers and ask them how else you should disseminate information about classes. It is possible that the local council, and within it the

Director of Public Health, may be able to provide information on the proportion of the population from different ethnic groups. We also know that some local authorities have approached church groups about teaching English to community organisations.

...try typing 'What's on in Exeter (replace with your city/town/village)' to see where you can add your listing for free online or in local publications.

...if you have a local university or college of further education, ask how to get in touch with any international student befriending groups. In the UK, the excellent Friends International is a Christian organisation which seeks to reach international students and is active in many areas (see resources later).

...if there is a specific nationality group you hope to attract, consider translating the publicity into the target language and post publicity in community centres and other venues like specialist food shops that tend to cater to specific nationalities. Hand car washes are another possible starting point.

...can you get your church to add a page on the church website? If possible, the page title (and URL) should contain the words 'free English classes' so the page will show up better in a search engine, such as Google.

...if you are up to date with social media, consider posting your new programme on Facebook (via your church group page or through a personal page) or using other social media outlets as you feel appropriate.

Tip: Keep a list of where you have posted information for future reference so you don't duplicate efforts. If you change any details, such as class times, you'll have an easy way to ensure all the publicity gets amended.

In any publicity, be clear about what you offer. Think about who your English classes are for. Are your classes aimed at all English levels or just beginners? Is it both men and women who will come or is it more likely to be one or the other? What are the times, days, and duration of classes? This may also impact on attendance.

Be sure to mention a friendly welcome and any extras such as a crèche, if you can offer that facility. Will you be using the Bible as a basis for lessons? If so, it is important to say so. Equally, if you will not be using the Bible but concentrating on general English themes, then make that clear. Some nationalities may be suspicious of your motives otherwise and will stay away from lessons. (We will come back to this area of whether to use the Bible in classes later on in Chapter 6.)

In any publicity, explain the benefits to your potential learners. These may seem obvious but it pays to spell this out.

These are just some ways you can publicise upcoming classes for your local programme, but it isn't an exhaustive list.

As we conclude this part on how to publicise your programme, let's look at an example of what you could put up on a noticeboard. On the following page there is an example of a free classes poster you could use:

<u>Free</u> English classes

Do you need to speak better English? We can help:

Improve your English for everyday communication

Practise speaking English in a safe environment

Build confidence

Meet new people

Lessons are completely free

We are friendly and welcome people of all levels, nationalities, and faiths. Tea, coffee and biscuits provided too ☺.

At: Our Church, Our Road, Our city

On: Thursdays 1.30pm – 3.00pm

For more information:

Programme co-ordinator (telephone number) or (email address)

No need to book, just come along. We look forward to welcoming you.

Recruiting volunteers

So, we have looked at how you might make people aware of the new programme you are setting up. But you will almost certainly need someone to help.

We know it's not always easy to ask people to do things. People are busy and perhaps we perceive they think we are just being a nuisance or that somehow we are going to *guilt-trip* them into helping.

As we have already said, your first port of call should be your church leaders who can advise on who may have time on their hands or who may be a good fit for the project.

Don't be discouraged if you get a few '*no's'* from those you invite initially. In our experience, many Christians are busy people and may be committed to a range of projects, both inside and outside church life. Similarly, some church members may be a little scared of signing up to new ventures either because they are concerned about the amount of time they will really need to devote to get it off the ground or because they don't see the vision at the moment.

If that is the case, don't worry unduly. Pray and then keep praying. If no-one seems especially keen, keep the vision but be prepared to start smaller. Just one other person to walk alongside, share the ups and downs, keep you accountable, pool ideas, and encourage you could be all that is needed to begin.

Once an operation is running and visible, you will probably find others will step forward. So be specific about why you are asking particular volunteers (their gifts, their personality, etc.) and what you want from them – and the expected time commitment. Ask face to face; you may be surprised by an enthusiastic response.

If someone needs to consider and get back to you, that's fine. Say you'll follow up by email outlining the vision, what you'd like them to do, and the expected time commitment and ask them to pray it through. But do it gently and ask for a response by a certain time.

Tip: List everything you feel needs to be done and break down the tasks into manageable chunks, so no single individual feels overwhelmed.

To build a bit of momentum behind the ESL idea, could you organise an ideas breakfast, a seminar on English language teaching, or speak at the front of church?

It sometimes helps to have a launch date as a focus and deadline for initial volunteer sign-ups. You can then update your church with progress updates, how many days to go until launch, and what you still need people to do. Provide a sign-up sheet on the notice board for the essential volunteer roles you would like filled.

Have a look at the list below for an idea of what you could post on your church noticeboard:

Volunteers needed example poster:

Can you help?

Free English classes launching at this church Thurs July 15th

Volunteers needed Thursdays to:

* Make tea & welcome
new people (1-1.45pm)
or
* Help in class (1.30-3.15pm)
or
Can you distribute publicity in a few spare
moments?
Sign up below by June 30th latest

Contact: Programme co-ordinator (telephone
number) or (email address)

Volunteer roles

There may just be one or two of you starting this venture and that is fine. However, the churches we have approached about their English language classes say volunteers are key to the success of the project. One person can coordinate and take a lead in the lessons but without volunteers, it is hard to keep things going, establish relationships, and provide the 'extras' that can make all the difference to the experience and welcome.

Volunteers can engage with your students in a number of ways.

If you have some keen volunteers and want to know how best to deploy them, here are some key volunteer roles but don't worry, you don't need all these to get things started.

…they could be assistants in lessons – helping with English in the lesson, in group work or 1-1, or you might have a TEFL/TESOL-trained teacher in your midst who wouldn't mind acting as a lead tutor.

…then try to engage some befrienders – a person or people to take an active interest/follow-up outside class.

…you could always benefit from a crèche organiser or helper, as well as an administrator – someone to help out with photocopying lessons or posting updates etc. on church noticeboards, drawing up a volunteer rota, publicising course dates, linking with outside agencies, publicity updates, resource finding, etc.

…finally, just someone to help out with the tea and coffee or to be on duty to welcome students to the class.

All these are roles that can be filled by volunteers and will really help you turn your vision into a reality.

As an example, on the following page you'll find a brief role description which you could hand out, detailing responsibilities for any teaching assistants or helpers.

It provides an idea of the level of commitment expected.

Teaching Assistant Volunteer Role

Helper needed to:

Assist lead teacher in classes.
Lead small groups, as directed by the main teacher.
Be ready to share your faith in the simplest way possible when appropriate.
Be friendly, professional, and a signpost learner to other church events/outside agencies as appropriate.
Pray regularly for this ministry.
Flag up any issues the lead tutor should be aware of, e.g. health and safety.
Commit to the 3 terms of 10 weeks over the year.
Arrange for someone to take my classes if I am not available.
Be available for 15 minutes after class for prayer and feedback.

Desirable: to consider TEFL workshop/training.

Programme Objectives

So, we've outlined ways to reach the community and you now have a few volunteers who have expressed an interest in helping. You have set a location, time, and date for your first class. What next?

Well, you will also need to think about what you aim to achieve in the classes. Set some clear objectives and provide a solid but semi-flexible framework that can adapt to changing needs and can be refined and improved as you go along.

After prayer, the first step might be to meet with relevant teaching members of the group to discuss and set your objectives. Then clearly communicate this to all volunteers so you are all pulling in the same direction.

Ensure that your plan/vision:

...unites everyone around a common purpose and stops issues down the line, such as, 'I thought our focus was...?'.

...stops people going off on their own agenda (e.g. I've also wanted to tackle the Chinese about their human rights record...).

...focuses attention on what is necessary (to meet the objective) and what goes on the 'would be nice to...' list.

At this point, it is good to think about what the

overall objective of the project is. It could be quite different, depending on a range of circumstances. Take a look at the following sample objectives:

Sample objectives

Here are some sample objectives. Think about which might best fit with your church English teaching programme:

…To help local immigrants to improve their English, to build confidence, help integration, and so improve lives and society. Ultimately to bring new people into God's family and find welcome as part of the church congregation.

…To show Christ practically by serving through English language teaching, being helpful and treating people with compassion. To look for creative ways to sensitively share the gospel - when appropriate and provide a safe and non-threatening learning environment.

…To help our church members understand English better, primarily so they can understand the sermons so we can make Jesus known and disciple them and get alongside.

You can imagine how a lesson's content may be different for each of the above. It is important to ensure the vision is understood, agreed, and shared amongst all your volunteers. So, check in regularly with volunteers to see if classes, follow-ups, etc. are meeting objectives and what might need to change. This does not need to be a big meeting; 15 minutes after class could be all that is needed to feedback, pray, and plan the next lesson in line with the objectives. Again, we will look a little more at this later in the chapter on retaining students in Chapter 6.

Getting the best out of volunteers

If you are the organiser, do remember to praise volunteers and send thank you cards/emails when it is due.

Have a social to bond occasionally. Share 'success stories' and 'breakthroughs' with the group. Prayer is crucial for any ministry and so pray for your students, volunteers, and the programme.

If possible, feed prayer updates and stories into your church life – through prayer letters etc. to encourage the wider congregation to pray for you and to invite those interested to get involved.

We are all prone to getting weary and Christians are not immune to this. The excitement at the beginning of a new project can soon ebb once routine sets in. Part of your role, if you are the leader, will be to encourage people to carry on, use their gifts, and grow into the roles God has given them.

We hope that this chapter has given you some useful ideas and suggestions for recruiting volunteers, creating publicity, and engaging with your church. You will find a list of Christian training courses, ELT networks, support agencies, and forums on the following further resources page.

Now, it starts to get exciting as we turn to our next chapter to look at simple ways to structure lessons and lesson content.

Further Resources for Getting Started

Teacher training courses, networking, support, forums:

1. Christian TEFL
Accredited online TEFL training courses for Christians:
Courses from 70-250 hours, plus CPD for already trained teachers:
www.christiantefl.org

2. Global English TESOL
Accredited online TESOL courses and short weekend courses. Sister organisation to Christian TEFL, over 20 years' experience in distance-based TEFL training:
www.global-english.com

3. Friends International's Teaching English Network Facebook group
https://www.facebook.com/groups/TENetwork/

4. Two:nineteen
English teaching and outreach forum:
http://www.englishandoutreach.com/

5. ODILS, Plymouth
General English classes that focus on asylum seekers. Trinity TESOL courses in a Christian environment:
http://www.odils.com/index.php/en/

6. Bridges Language schools
Model documents, advice and support for those starting language schools in churches:
Courses from 70-250 hours, plus CPD for already

trained teachers:
http://www.twonineteen.org.uk/how-can-we-help/bridges/

7. Glasgow asylum seeker support project - PDF
A little dated, but easy to read and provides an interesting overview and case studies:
http://bit.ly/1kmwanO

CHAPTER 4

CREATING LESSONS

In this chapter...

We will start to look at how to create effective lessons that will enable your students to gain confidence in English and develop their grammar skills and fluency. We will also think about what we can teach them that will be most helpful for their learning situations, and then look at a couple of different ways of structuring your lessons.

All our lessons need some form of structure if they are to be effective. So let's start with this first.

How to structure your lessons

Before we look more specifically at what to teach, we're going to focus first on a couple of popular ways to organise your classes – particularly how you can structure and time the main lesson components.

We are going to look at two different ways of setting up your lessons. The following lesson plan structures are not set in stone - and a good TEFL course will provide more depth on lesson staging –

but the following are simple and effective ways to organise your classes.

You'll notice that both structures start with a simple introductory activity called a **warmer or engagement activity,** designed to get students warmed up to English. Then you will see that there is a period of **whole class** activity, followed by **group or pair work.** We will look at why this is a good idea later.

Both the following class organisation patterns are based on a 1.5-hour class (1.5 - 2 hours seems a popular duration), so take a look at the different structures on the following pages.

You will note that there is a suggested time next to each one but that this can be very flexible, depending on your situation.

Class organisation pattern A:

Welcome, tea/coffee (10 mins)

Whole class introduction communicative game or activity (10 mins)
Why: to warm learners up to English & lessen inhibitions around speaking in front of others or making mistakes.

Teacher leads class from front (15 mins)
Why: to introduce the theme, any new language, and to practise as a class.

Follow-up activity/worksheet (25 mins)
Why: for a concentrated practice of the new language in groups or pairs with the assistance of a volunteer, then get feedback /discuss any issues as a class.

Optional additions after the main class (30 mins)
Bible study in English
or
More individual help with form filling, literacy, specific questions etc.

Class organisation pattern B:

Whole class intro communication game or activity (5 mins)

Further communicative games and activities as a class (25 mins)

Group work, depending on needs and number of volunteers (60 mins)

For example:
Beginners work on writing/literacy/form filling, higher levels focus on English for work.

As we mentioned before, both structures start with a short introductory activity called a ***warmer.*** Let's look at some of these in more detail next.

Warmers

A warmer is a simple introductory engagement task in English. Think of a game of **hangman** or **Simon says**, and you have the idea.

If you look back at the two different class structures on the previous page, you will notice that we suggest using games or communication activities at the beginning of the class. As we said, these are designed to get learners warmed up to English.

Here are some reasons why you might want to start with some fun, engaging, and simple English tasks or games:

...warmers, like Simon says, help learners commence speaking English so they lose some of their inhibitions about talking in English in front of the class.

...they are simple (so not off-putting) and get people smiling and joining in easily.

...they can link the introductory activities to the theme of the class to really good effect.

Now let's move on to look at some specific lesson ideas that can work well across a range of different classes.

Lesson idea 1

Here is an example of a warmer that illustrates the final reason above.

Imagine the theme of the lesson is focused on giving personal details, such as being able to spell out names, email addresses, phone numbers etc.

Your warmer could be: give each student a letter of the alphabet. Then, dictate one word at a time, getting students to arrange themselves accordingly at the front of the class so they spell the word you have dictated.

If you are looking for ideas for activities for your classes to get them warmed up, think about some of the following. You might remember them from school, they still work…

Here is a list of simple games we have used successfully:

…Simon says

…I went to the market and I bought…

This is a memory chain where each person, in turn, says the words above, adding an item to the growing list.

…Who am I?

Stick the name of a famous person to the back of each student. Students have to mingle with each other asking only **yes/no questions** to find out who they are. Examples might be: 'Am I alive? Am I a woman? Am I a politician?' etc. You can see an example of this in action here:

https://youtu.be/z1je387GJmw

…Quizzes and questionnaires

Have teams compete to answer questions based on corrections from previous lessons.

Here is the beginning of a class questionnaire on likes and dislikes as an example. They can either devise their own class questionnaire or, for ease, you could give them a chart, as below (with all the words in black given). Students then go around the room and ask each other questions such as, in this case, *'do you like bananas?'*, and putting a mark in the appropriate box and reporting back on the most popular food.

Food: Bananas - Like 3, Dislike 2

Food: Marmalade - Like 1, Dislike 3

Food: Lemons - Like 2, Dislike 4

…Chants and songs

Sing together with lyrics, then take the words away.

…Board relays

If you haven't seen these before, then here is how

they work.

Divide the class into two teams. The first member of each team runs to the board to unscramble an anagram (or other board activity) and then runs back to hand the pen on to the next member of the team, who runs to the board and repeats the same process for the next anagram. The first team to unscramble all the anagrams wins.

...Board activities

If you have small groups, bring them up to the board and have them do an activity. This could be a matching activity or a writing activity where they have to think of answers to questions and then write them on the board.

Here is an example of a slightly different board game in a TEFL lesson:

https://youtu.be/8Fyl2ZwEWpY

So these are just a few ideas of activities to engage your students. These will help them to get **warmed up** to English and ready for what you are about to teach them.

This is where we are heading next. So let's look now at what comes after our warmer activity as we go on to look at whole class activities, group and pair work.

Whole class activities, group and pair work

Look back again to the two different class structures we outlined earlier in Chapter 3.

As well as introductory warmers, did you notice that both patterns included whole class time (with the teacher leading from the front) with smaller group or pair work as follow-ups?

There are some good reasons why you might want to include whole class time first, followed up by smaller group work after. We will look at why next.

A whole class activity is where the entire class is engaged together in the same activity with the tutor leading/playing an active role.

We try to do this because it enables the teacher to set a theme, to engage the whole class, and set a strong context for the language to occur. It also means, crucially, that the tutor can deal with any difficulties students may have with the new language or new concepts together as a class - before students go off into smaller groups/pairs to practise the language further.

In short, you don't want students practising mistakes.

Let's have a look at an example of how this might work.

Lesson idea 2

Here is an idea for a real lesson, based on shopping for everyday items. Imagine the theme for a low-level English class is asking for grocery items in shops. Firstly, the teacher could bring in food items for the whole class to handle and name, such as:

bread, milk, eggs, butter, sugar, cheese, apples, bananas.

The teacher names each item as he/she holds it up for the class to repeat.

Then each item could be passed between students with the students saying the name of each item as they pass it on.

The teacher can test retention by holding an item up and asking individual students to name it.

Moving on, the teacher could then role-play a simple dialogue in front of the class. The teacher would act as a customer with one of the volunteers acting as a shopkeeper. The teacher asks for the items using simple phrases and repeating them.

The teacher would model phrases like:

"Please can I have some…?"

"Here you are." (hands over item)

"Thank you."

After a couple of turns, the teacher then replaces the volunteer with individual class members, replicating the simple dialogue in front of the class, prompting as necessary.

The teacher may then elicit the correct dialogue, line by line, from the class to write on the board, so the class has a model dialogue to take home and practise.

Can you see the benefits of the whole class being involved like this? In this way, everyone is engaged in the theme and the teacher can explain and model the key language points to the whole group, setting the scene and providing the essential vocabulary and phrases needed for the class from the start.

What next?

You have modelled the target structure and language. You have been able to correct any issues and target difficult to pronounce words as a class. A few of the braver students have got up to have a go (hopefully!).

However, you want to ensure every individual has a chance to practise the target language more than once so they can build confidence in using these useful phrases.

Well, this is where working together in pairs or

small groups is a useful follow-up to the whole class lead-in.

So, let's look at some of the advantages of small group/pair work follow-ups next.

Working in pairs or small groups enables practice to occur simultaneously. Since everyone can be practising at the same time (instead of one at a time in front of the class), this means more practice time for everyone – and more practice time for students is a good thing.

Lesson idea 3

Let's examine how this works by following on from the lesson example in the last chapter on asking for things in shops. A great pair work follow-up idea would be to get students to practise the dialogue together, taking it in turns to be the customer. They could do this multiple times, asking for different items. You and your volunteers circulate to help with structure and pronunciation.

This is great as it provides students with plenty of practice of everyday, useful conversations. They can practise safely in a supportive and friendly environment. All this great practice will hopefully mean your students will have more confidence in using this English in real life.

This was a very simple lesson for low-level

learners. Using the same basic structure, you could extend the dialogues depending on the level of your learners. Activities you could include in similar lessons might be:

...opening a bank account
...ordering a meal in a restaurant
...asking for a prescription to be filled at a chemist
...going to the post office to transfer money

Or have the learners tell you what they need to do. This can help to ensure that the lessons are relevant to your classes.

There are some additional advantages to pair work and group work. Let's look at these below.

Benefits of pair and group work

...enables learners with similar needs to work together
...volunteers can get to know individuals better
...enables learners to work with other learners at their level
...encourages shy members of the class to speak and get involved

We hope that the above has given you some clear and simple ways to plan your classes.

Essentially both the structures that we have looked at follow a similar pattern:

…warmer
…whole class activity/teaching
…plenty of practice of the language in groups or pairs

It is not essential to follow this structure every time, but if you are looking for a simple, effective way to structure classes, this works well. Now, let's move on to look at what to teach.

"I put the syllabus together as I wanted the classes to cover functional English e.g. greetings, weather, money, shopping, time, calendar etc." (James Myles, WPCA, Belfast)

What to teach

Some groups teaching English in church concentrate on listening and speaking only, which they see as integral for faster community integration. Others teach a blend of the four skills (listening, reading, speaking and writing). Others look to focus on functional English for everyday needs within the community.

Some invest in course books (see resources for popular EFL titles - you can often get copies second hand from Amazon/eBay etc.) but most use a range of resources, sourced from the internet, resource books, and even create their own. But before you spend precious resources on an expensive set of course books and related materials, it would be wise to find out <u>why</u> your students are seeking to learn English. This could be discovered by something as informal as having students discuss their needs together in class.

When you commence your lessons, consider writing the following prompts on the board in the first lesson as a guide to work from:

Why do you need English?
Do you prefer reading, writing, listening, speaking, or grammar?
What do you find difficult in English?
What do you hope to learn in the classes?

You might like to put your students in pairs to ask their partner questions about their English based on the above prompts, or you could do this as a simple quiz or questionnaire. For very low-level groups, if you have someone who can translate for you, this could be worthwhile.

Afterwards, get them to write down their responses in note form and hand them to you, so that you have an idea of the needs and wants of your class.

It is interesting that many of the EFL teachers we asked said that their students respond best to lessons that are both enjoyable and interactive, often with a focus on speaking. This makes sense when you think about it. For example, how would you prefer to learn Spanish, German or another language? I expect you would like a teacher to make learning engaging and to encourage you to participate actively in the lessons.

When people are smiling and enjoying activities, they are more likely to participate and return. So we suggest making your lessons as engaging as possible.

Let's look at some ways that we can focus on speaking activities, with a few ideas for how to do it, and some potential pitfalls to avoid.

Speaking activities

Ask the majority of English language students in the UK what they want to focus on in class and they will mostly say **speaking**. Most students want to focus on being understood and communicating clearly in English.

We would still use written text or audio to stimulate ideas, provide a context, and to introduce some key language, but in general church-based English classes, it seems reading and writing are rarely the main focus in lessons.

Great, speaking....so let's just chat? What would you think about starting a class with the following:

Today we're going to discuss – are circuses cruel? Ok – go…

Well, if you started your class in the above way, we suspect you'd likely be met with a lot of blank faces. The writer of this should know, as early in his teaching career, he commenced a general English class with just that phrase. It didn't go well!

So, if we take the above approach, we are likely to fail as, firstly, students are not warmed up and there is no context, lead-in or helpful language given to support the theme.

Secondly, there is no particular outcome to work towards and no specific purpose or task. In addition, students are going into the activity 'cold' without any parameters, guidelines or time to think about the subject.

As a contrast, good speaking activities for the ESL classroom have an end result in mind, along with a context around which to frame the activity, so there is a meaningful purpose to communicating. So, let's look at some speaking activities that work best.

Here are a few ideas.

Communication activities

There are many useful communication activities and here are a few of our favourites that we have seen work well in a setting where you have students from a variety of backgrounds and cultures.

Practical communication activities where you simulate or role-play can be very useful activities.

From going to the bank to open an account, or a visit to the doctor or dentist, even having a job interview can provide a framework for meaningful language practice.

Be sure to provide some useful language before they start – or provide the outline of a sample dialogue which they can extend so they have something to use to help and prompt. Let's look at one simple idea next.

Lesson idea 4

What's wrong? Going to the doctor's

Bring in *realia* (or real objects) to help set a context and make the new vocabulary come alive. For example, a bandage, plasters and medicine. Or even a stethoscope (if you can get hold of one).

Start by brainstorming parts of the body. Then have students match parts of the body to the correct potential ailment on the board and potential cure. For example:

Leg/arm ---- broken/sprain
Head/stomach ---- ache/hurt/pain
Bandage ---- medicine ---- x-ray ---- hospital

Next, mime the following:

Limp, doubling over, holding stomach etc.

Have the students tell you what is wrong with you, for example:

"Your arm might be broken. You should go for an x-ray."

Then put students into pairs and have them do the same mime/prescribed exercise together. Next, have them mime something else and give the relevant advice.

This type of activity can be adapted to be realistic and relevant to the communities you are teaching. Learners will really appreciate the opportunities to practise and hopefully will see the relevance of the lesson.

You can build a more in-depth dialogue on the board, miming to elicit each line and refining the phrases.

Lesson idea 5

Job interviews

Bring a simple job advert and discuss it as a class. Ensure they know what any difficult vocabulary means, such as 'part-time'.

Then, split the class into **employers** and **employees** with each group coming up with potential questions or potential answers respectively. Go around the room and correct to ensure that the examples they are using are correct.

Next, line up everyone in the employer group with someone from the employee group, allowing them a few minutes to ask or answer some questions. After a couple of minutes, move the employee on to the next employer until each employer has interviewed each employee. How well did the potential employees answer? Ask the employers who they would employ and why. Go over some of the best responses at the front of the class and say why they might work effectively if learners find themselves in this situation.

This can give some invaluable experience to students who may be looking for work as they can benefit from some real practice of interview questions.

Consensus-seeking activities

This generally involves getting individual students to prioritise a list of items. They then have to talk to a partner and try to come up with a new, agreed list between them, justifying and negotiating. This can be adapted for a range of themes, such as most important qualities in a partner or major issues the world will face in five years' time.

These ideas can lead on to interesting discussions which you can develop.

Information gaps

Another type of task where speaking can be encouraged is an information gap activity.

Here, student A has some information that has to be given to student B to complete the whole picture/puzzle.

For example, Student A draws an outline of their room and places the main items of furniture in it (a bed, desk, chair etc.). Then they describe the room to a partner, for example:

"There is a desk in the corner of the room."

Student B has to draw the room, based on student A's description. At the end of the exercise, they compare drawings. It is great for practising prepositions of place: next to, opposite, in front of, in, on, under, etc. It can also be adapted easily to describe a street, where students place the school, post office, bank or hairdresser's, etc.

Debates

Debates can be interesting, particularly if you have more advanced groups.

We suggest choosing neutral topics (such as global warming or something local, such as transport or parking) and help your students by providing time in groups to come up with arguments for or against, before allowing them to debate. However, it is best to stick to neutral topics and do be aware of any cultural sensitivities specific to the groups you are teaching.

"Cover topics that will be relevant to them, e.g. renting, finding a job, food shopping, travel. Find relevant speakers e.g. nurse, health trainer, Citizens Advice Bureau etc." (Sue Wood, Belmont Church, Exeter)

Quizzes/questionnaires

Students can create questions around a theme and ask their partners. For example, if your students need to practise completing forms for everyday things like a bank account or an online registration for a website, collect some real ones and have one student ask the other for information and complete the form with their partner. This is great practice for giving, receiving, and recording personal information and mirrors what they may have to do in real life.

Dialogue building

With a class volunteer, role-play a short, easy dialogue in which you ask someone to the cinema or to go for a coffee, for example.

Write prompts from the dialogue on the board afterwards, e.g.:

Free Sunday?
Restaurant? Burger King? 7.30 p.m.?
Café on the corner? Costa Coffee?
Skinny latte?

Cinema Saturday?
Avengers or Hulk?
Meeting inside at 4pm?

Let pairs use the prompts to create full sentences orally, role-playing with their partner. As you go around the class monitoring, you might hear dialogues like the following:

Student A: "Are you free Sunday?
Student B: Sure.
Student A: Shall we go to Burger King?
Student B: Yes. What time?
Student A: Let's meet inside at 4?
Student B: Ok. See you then."

So, let's summarise where we have got up to thus far. In this chapter, we have looked at what to teach and focused specifically on speaking or communication activities, providing you with some ideas that you can use in your classes. We hope that these are helpful!

Don't forget that learners may still need help with writing, reading and listening, so these speaking activities may be part of lessons that include a blend of skills practice. However, our focus has been on producing useful and meaningful spoken English through engaging tasks, as we think this will be of most use to you in your teaching.

Creating lessons summary

We hope that this chapter has been helpful for you as you start to look at how to create effective and structured lessons.

There is a wealth of resources available to help you with this – we have listed just a few of the ones that we have found to be useful in the further resources chapter on the next page. You will also find a comprehensive list of additional resources for all chapters at the end of this guide in Chapter 8.

Further Resources of Creating Lessons

General English learning resources ready to print or buy:

1. 50 conversation classes
See a free 35-page sample online here:
http://bit.ly/1M5f4Hk
An inexpensive hard copy is also available on Amazon.

2. ESOL lesson plans
Free online - just select the level and skill you want to practise at the Skills Workshop site:
http://www.skillsworkshop.org/esol

3. iteslj
Hundreds of free ready to use discussion topics and questions organised by theme at the iteslj site:
http://iteslj.org/questions/

4. Breaking News English
Online, free news items arranged by level. You can listen, read and do the exercises:
http://www.breakingnewsenglish.com/

5. OnestopEnglish
Online, free monthly news items arranged by level with useful post-reading exercises and answer key:
http://bit.ly/1m2L0ze

6. ESOL Activities
Photocopiable lessons. Entry level 1 Book with audio CD. Look inside on the Amazon site. Also available - level 2 & 3:

http://amzn.to/1ZUcY1a

7. Handouts Online
Access hundreds of ready to use plans for a very cheap yearly subscription:
http://handoutsonline.com/

8. English Grammar in Use
Fantastic book resource for the teacher: simple grammar explanations, exercises and answer key. Such a popular title, you should easily be able to order second-hand:
http://amzn.to/1XhLDDP

9. Your English Source
ESOL photocopiables, task sheets and teacher notes for field trips like 'at the grocery store' or 'cooking.' Try 3 free and download 40 such lessons for between $5 and $15.
http://yourenglishsource.com/activity-based/

10. iSLCollective
Free ESL printables made by teachers from iSLCollective. You'll need to sign-up as a member, then download for free:
https://en.islcollective.com/resources/printables

CHAPTER 5

TEACHING ENGLISH TO BEGINNERS

If we say someone is a *beginner* in English, maybe a few assumptions come to mind about that learner.

Before we go further, have a look at the following.

Which statements do you agree with?

True or False? A beginner in English is defined as someone who:

a) cannot write in our Roman script
b) is illiterate in their own language
c) cannot speak any English whatsoever

Well, all of them could be true! Equally, none of them might apply.

That's because beginners are not a homogenous group. Certainly, a beginner in English will not be able to function in English well, their performance in English may be patchy. Perhaps they can understand a fair bit but can only read and speak very little, if anything. Some of your beginners may have hardly held a pen before, whereas others will be able to write well in their own language – but if they are not familiar with the Roman script, they will

61

struggle to read and write in English.

Teaching beginners, especially those with low levels of literacy in English (who struggle to read and write for whatever reason) can be very challenging. There is little to 'hang' a lesson on and the teacher will need to consider how they present and explain everything. However, there are some great up-sides too. If they are a beginner, then the sense of achievement in going from 0-10 words is immense and can lead to great levels of motivation.

While we can't go into great depth here, we have listed some ideas to get you started with beginners and found some excellent resources for you to try out if you have beginners in your classes. For ease, these ideas are mostly intended for beginners who cannot speak, read or write much English but do have experience with the Roman script.

Additionally, at the end of this chapter, there is a link to lesson plans for zero or low levels of writing ability in English (see resource no. 6 which links to 10 lessons for beginners for just such learners).

So let's start to take a look at teaching English to beginners.

Understanding comes first

When your beginners can soon follow basic spoken instructions in English, such as: stand up, sit down, pick up your pen, talk to your partner, this is good news. They may not be able to produce this language themselves but understanding is the first step to becoming familiar with the language and interacting meaningfully in English.

So, think of a few instructions you will regularly use in your class, which they will hear again and again. These might be:

pick up your pen
talk to your partner
listen, tell, ask, speak, repeat
draw, write, highlight, underline
stand up
sit down

At first, you will need to accompany these instructions with an appropriate mime but after a while, you can just say the words. You will be surprised how much language can be understood this way – even when these repeated instructions are not the focus of the lesson.

Lesson idea 6

Stand by the door and as each student comes in say:

"Welcome...please sit down."

(Big smile, arms outstretched for "welcome", or a

handshake. Point to a chair for "please sit down".) By the time the last student comes in, many in class will have heard this phrase several times and will know what it means.

Next class, you can drop the mime and just say the words. You can even station a student by the door and get them to do the welcoming for you.

Using repetition

Just as repeating "Welcome...please sit down" works, hearing any phrase plenty of times (and then getting the chance to repeat it plenty of times) is the best way for beginners to understand and then produce the language.

So, with beginners, your main job as the teacher is to select useful language - and then give students plenty of opportunities to hear and repeat this language - again, and again and again.

It's important not to introduce too much language as this will be too overwhelming. For complete beginners, 6-8 new vocabulary items and 4-6 phrases per lesson are potentially enough for one class.

You can see this in the second lesson idea mentioned in the previous chapter **(Creating**

lessons that work) on buying grocery items in a shop. Did you notice how many words and phrases were introduced? Not many. Instead, most of the lesson was spent on students learning the new vocabulary and phrases and practising them again and again in different tasks.

Repeating after the teacher word by word or line by line is called **Drilling**. It can be very effective at lower levels. Recycle language in lessons regularly as practice makes perfect and encourage your students to practise at home.

Repeating and repeating can be quite dull so keep it moving and think of other ways to recycle. You could use flash cards (See #8 in further resources at the end of this chapter), chop up sentences for them to reconstruct, and conduct quizzes in teams based on past material.

Appropriate language for beginners

If you can, ask them in their first language what they want to be able to say or get someone to translate it for you. Teach useful things first. You may be tempted to teach numbers 1-100, the alphabet, colours, etc. After all, this seems somehow logical and concrete. However, these are not tremendously functional.

Certainly, learning numbers 1-10 is useful - students can give and receive phone numbers and begin to understand the words for the money in their pockets. Similarly, being able to spell your own name is handy.

However, what is most useful is having some language for functional and meaningful communication. This may be for the shops, the doctor, calling a child's school, giving personal information; all the things you would like to know as soon as possible if you were living overseas and English was not spoken.

So, think about building simple dialogues with your beginner learners, repeating line by line.

Don't break down/analyse language too much; teach useful 'functional' phrases as a chunk.

Here are a few examples:

Expressing opinions:
"I like… I don't like…"

Labelling:
"It's a… This is a…"

Asking for permission:
"Can I open the window?"

Greetings:
"Nice to meet you… How are you..."

Giving personal information:
"I live in… I've got three children… my name is…"

Dialogues and useful phrases: language for shopping, the doctor, etc.

Lesson idea 7

Here is a great technique for giving personal information. It involves drawing pictures on the board that show your life - while you tell the story to accompany each picture, like in the following example.

Teacher draws a basic family tree diagram, adding names, and says while pointing to the pictures on the board:

"I am married to Tom. I've got two children. My son is called Jim and my daughter is called Lou."

The teacher says this aloud. The class repeats once or twice together. Teacher rubs out the words: Tom and Jim.

Class repeats the sentences.

The teacher rubs out more words. The class repeats and so on until the class can repeat the phrase with no word prompts.

Learners draw their own immediate relationships to explain to their partners. You may have to supply some extra vocabulary, e.g. I am not married, I have two sisters, etc. depending on your students' relationships. You could extend your story, depending on the capacity of your learners, including the name of your town, your job, your husband's job, and any other details.

Be visual

Can you imagine trying to tell your beginners about you, Tom, and your children (as in the example above) without the accompanying drawings?

Such visuals are helpful for all levels but especially for beginners. So where possible, show and don't just tell. Bring in real items, use flash cards, mime, and use picture stories.

Picture stories, in particular, are great for low-level learners since it is obvious what is happening in context with no language explanation necessary. Don't worry if you are not a great artist! As you will see from all the drawings in this chapter, simple stick figures are fine.

Now, here is another illustration of how to use a picture story. This uses the simple present tense: I go, I walk, etc. but sets these in the context of daily routines; an accessible theme everyone can relate to. Look at the picture story and read the instructions on the next page.

Lesson idea 8

...Brainstorm to begin. Students look at the picture story handout below and say as many words as they recognise.

...The teacher points to box 1 (top left corner) and says: "I get up..." (you can also mime this, too). Class repeats.

...Teachers says: "I get dressed..." (points to box 2) and the class repeats...and "I eat breakfast" (points to box 3)...and the class repeats again.

…Repeat the above process and then ask learners to repeat individually, pointing at either box 1, 2 or 3.

…Teacher repeats the process for box 4-6 and then 7-9.

…Get the students to cut up the pictures. Have one person in each pair hold all the pictures. They place one picture on the desk at random and their partner has to provide the accompanying statement. If the speaker is 100% correct, they keep the picture. How many of the 9 can they collect?

Reverse roles and repeat the activity. If students are interested, play a couple of times.

The teacher can help more advanced pairs to add in times like "I get up at 7 o'clock" for example. Or make it more natural sounding with "and then I…". By the end of the lesson, can the pairs say the whole story? If not, get them to practise at home for next time.

Alternatively, you could give students a picture story and the accompanying text and read it together a few times. To practise the language, they then cover the words and re-tell it to their partner using the very helpful visual prompts.

So far, so good. However, we have to admit the particular picture story we have used is not very functional. After all, who goes about reciting their daily routine? However, we couldn't resist including this exercise as there are some very useful, high-frequency verbs introduced, such as eat, go, and watch, which will be especially useful to low-level learners. Beginners often get a tremendous sense of achievement from being able to fluently tell a story and string words together.

A sample beginner curriculum

Up to now, we have looked at how using visual materials can help us teach beginners, how we might use repetition to good effect, and thought about the appropriate level of language. Now, what sort of curriculum or series of lessons should we be looking to teach towards? Hopefully, what follows, in the suggested sample beginner curriculum, might give you some good ideas.

A sample curriculum will vary depending on the needs of your students, but here are a few themes and language points for your first 15 or so classes, although this can be very flexible:

Class 1: Giving personal information/greetings, asking for personal information, spelling your name:
My name is…
I live in…
I'm from…
What's your name?
How are you?
That's spelt W I L L I A M…

Class 2: Asking for permission with useful verbs, asking for help:
"Can I…? smoke, sit here, open a window…"
"Can you help me…?"

Class 3: Numbers, including phone numbers:
1-10 or 1-20.

Class 4: Dealing with money:
"Three pounds twenty", "two dollars fifty…"

Class 5: Professions and everyday jobs:
"I'm a ….you're a……he's a……"

Class 6: Family and relationships:
"I've got three brothers, I haven't got any sisters…"

Class 7: Days of the week:
"Today is… Tomorrow is… Yesterday was…."

Class 8: Months of the year and the weather:
"It is cold in December…"

Class 9: Diary arrangements and time:
"Can we meet on Monday at 3 o'clock?"

Class 10: Everyday food items, asking for things in a shop:
"Bread, milk, chicken, fish, vegetables…"

Class 11: More food items, expressing likes and dislikes:
"I prefer fish, she's a vegetarian…"

Class 12: Fluency and everyday routines:

"I get up, I go to work..."

Class 13: Parts of the body, a visit to the doctors:
"Arm, leg, chest... I have a pain in my..."

Class 14: Directions and places:
"Turn left, then turn right, go straight on..."
"The library, the doctor's surgery, etc."

Class 15: Clothes/colours, including the present continuous:
"I'm wearing a black jacket..."

Again, this is just a suggested outline, which can be varied and customised to your students and their particular needs. Also, see the further resources at the end of this chapter for more examples of an outline curriculum, lesson plans, samples, and language points.

Finally, we've got a question for you to ponder...

As a beginner in an English-speaking country, is it better to acquire a lot of English imperfectly or is it better to try and master a small amount of English perfectly?

Well, ideally, we are looking to get our beginners to a point where they can have a go in English across a range of situations rather than have to wait for them to be perfect in a little English.

As a result, you'll see beginners need lots of vocabulary. So we suggest teaching high-frequency words, such as useful verbs like: be, have, go, see, listen, hear, write, speak…, and nouns, such as: he, she, it, they, we, I…alongside adjectives like: big, small, good, bad, difficult, easy…

which can be applied across lots of different functions.

A final word on teaching English to beginners

It takes a lot of concentration as a beginner. Everything is new. Help by changing activities, miming, keeping a good pace, and being energetic in the classroom so that their energy and enthusiasm for English doesn't flag. But if you do find energy flagging, feel free to use a 'warmer' to get things moving again.

Some learners have had poor learning experiences. So consider bolstering confidence with smiles, plenty of revision, and a *thumbs up* 'well done'.

We have found some excellent resources for you, which are listed below. Unfortunately, a lot of material for beginners is aimed at young children. We suggest avoiding materials that are targeted in this way as it can come across as very patronising to adults. So let's take a look at what's currently available as further resources.

Further resources for Teaching English to Beginners

1. Springinstitute.org
PDFs for teaching asylum seekers and refugees. E.g.: includes working with preliterate and non-literate learners:
https://www.springinstitute.org/esl-resources/

2. iteslj
One page overview on approaches at **iteslj.org**:
http://iteslj.org/Techniques/Andrews-Beginners.html

3. OnestopEnglish
Step-by-step 10 lessons for absolute beginners free online with teaching notes:
http://www.onestopenglish.com/esol/absolute-beginners/unit-2/
Each plan is split into 2: for learners with and without knowledge of the Roman script.

4. Excellence Gateway
Step-by-step curriculum for ESOL entry level 1, 2 and 3 (elementary, pre-intermediate and intermediate levels learners), some excellent beginner material: colourful and vivid but you have to click on a link to each individual unit, which is rather cumbersome:
http://esol.excellencegateway.org.uk/vocabulary/EGaudience/learning-materials

5. Minnesota Literacy Council
Simple ESL lessons for everyday activities. Free and online: at work, calling in sick to a child's school, at the clinic. Each lesson starts with pictures/photos to outline the concept. The story or

dialogue follows with questions underneath. Useful ideas at the start of the document and there is a sample plan at the end:
http://mnliteracy.org/sites/default/files/beginning_esl_story_bank.pdf

6. Skills workshop
Printable and ready-to-use lessons for ESOL classes. At the drop-down, select (E1 which is entry level, meaning low 'elementary' level – above beginner) and at the 'subject area' drop-down, select what you want to practise.
Some good lesson ideas with accompanying worksheets:
http://bit.ly/1W3v0id

7. Skills Workshop
100 most frequent words in alphabetical order:
http://www.skillsworkshop.org/resources/100-keywords-alphabetical-order

8. ESL flashcards
Free, downloadable and printable flashcards:
http://www.eslflashcards.com/

9. Pictures of English Tenses Elementary
View and download this book online:
http://bit.ly/1W2yz2G

INTERMISSION

THE ROLE OF THE TEACHER IN THE CLASSROOM

At this point, we thought it would be helpful to create a short summary of the role of the teacher in the classroom. We hope this will consolidate some of the ideas already introduced and extend them further, so you are maximising class time and being as effective as possible.

Start:

Arrange your class in a horseshoe shape to begin so everyone has equal access to the board and the teacher. It helps communication and means students cannot hide at the back. Students can move chairs for group and pair work.

Tell volunteers the role you would like them to play in assisting you/the learners.

Then:

Lead the class with a warmer and/or whole class activity that sets the scene, engages, and introduces the key language or concepts they'll need.

Then:

Check students have the key language necessary for the task or provide it for them.

For example, explain any difficult vocabulary from their reading text before they read. This will help the reading 'flow', stop them getting distracted by unknown words, and ensure you need only explain these terms once as a class rather than multiple times to individuals.

Then:

Set pair/group work tasks to follow on from the whole class activity which are meaningful/have an end purpose. See 'what to teach' chapter. Allow plenty of student talking/communication time.

Remember:

Always correct mistakes but <u>sensitively</u>. While students are talking, you can monitor unobtrusively, taking notes to correct together as a class at the end of an activity. You might write up the mistakes and elicit the correct answer from the class.

Encourage students to use English outside of class as one meeting with you per week will not transform their English; instead, classes should be seen as a stimulus for real use. So, give students something meaningful to do in between English classes. If possible, have them report back next time (this really focuses the mind.) They might interview their family in English or start a discussion in a shop. It might be writing up a dialogue they had in class/home. as consolidation. When they use their new English in 'real life', it can be really motivating.

New Teacher tip: Make sure your students are talking more than you so they get to practise English. Explain, set a task or series of tasks, and step back while they complete them in groups or pairs to maximise speaking/practice time.

CHAPTER 6

TEACHING ENGLISH IN CHURCH CHALLENGES

So far, so good. We know that what we have covered so far may well have prompted several questions. There are a number of challenges to teaching English to learners in a church setting, and before we progress further, it would be worthwhile to look at some of these and how we can overcome them. We'll look specifically at how we can keep our students coming to classes, how we can keep our learners central to our teaching, and then go on to explore when it's right to move from teaching English to sharing the gospel. We'll tackle the question of whether we should use the Bible in our classes and gain some advice from those in the field already engaging in this form of ministry.

Let's get started on how we can keep our students coming back for lessons.

Retaining students

Have you ever started an evening class - perhaps you decided to delve into a new language like French or Spanish, or thought you'd have a go at

Art or something practical? Yet, you found enthusiasm waning as the term progressed?

Keeping motivated to attend with all of life's distractions can be difficult for even the keenest.

Lack of motivation is a key issue for church-based ESL classes, too. There could, of course, be a whole host of other reasons why learners drop out. It might be due to a change of circumstance or other competing issues in the learners' lives. However, there are some key ways we can do our bit to help trainees keep coming, learning, and enjoying classes. Let's look at some of these now.

Let's begin by looking at 6 ideas that will help you retain students. You can pick and choose what might work best for you.

1) Set term dates (an eight to ten week programme is a popular framework) or Spring, Summer, and Autumn terms may work best. This makes classes seem less like a 'drop-in over the year' type effort. Volunteers and learners get some breathing space and can gear up again for the next course.

2) Consider setting a registration date for all new learners to sign up ahead of the first class. Here you can take contact details for follow-ups and can get an idea of level and needs. People can register in person at the church or by email.

3) Try to follow up when a learner fails to attend more than one lesson. It is nice to be missed! It is

also a good chance to ask for feedback on lessons and what may have changed in their life. An email, phone call or postcard is all that is needed.

4) Consider whether it is appropriate to set a small fee. £1 a lesson is popular – this might be paid up-front for the course at registration. People tend to value what they have paid for and are more likely to attend as a result.

However, there are very good reasons for keeping lessons entirely free as well. One church English language teaching project we know keeps the lessons free but asks for a contribution for refreshments.

Alternatively, if you have decided to follow a course book, you could ask each student to purchase their own.

5) Create a professional ethos in class that learners will respect. Try keeping to time yourself and planning effective lessons, doing the simple housekeeping things like the register or ensuring enough photocopies are ready, etc.

Have a few rules for the class. This could be turning mobiles off or everyone agreeing to try and be on time so class disruption is minimised. An English only in-class policy could be helpful if that's appropriate, although if you are teaching beginners or elementary learners, it may be that some mother tongue help is needed.

6) Finally, ensure you get some feedback. Before your volunteer helpers leave, take a few minutes at the end of the class and ask for feedback under the following headings:

WWW or What **W**ent **W**ell

EBI or **E**ven **B**etter **I**f…

Always ask and expect feedback in this way so it soon becomes a habit (even if it is strange at first). It will also give volunteers an opportunity to feed in any specific information on learners who have had difficulties.

In this post-lesson slot, you can pray, give some information or discuss ideas for the next lesson and suggest who might follow up with attendees that have missed more than one class.

However, the main aim of this feedback time is to reflect on what went well, what could be better and then to act on this for future lessons to begin a continuous cycle of improvement.

It's not always easy to ask *"How do you think that went?"* at the end of a class if you are leading, but honest feedback is essential because we don't want any obstacles to reaching people effectively. We also want to communicate to our learners (and to our volunteers) that we take our role seriously and that we are striving to create professional lessons - that we are creative, trying out different methods in order to best meet needs.

One of the key ways to ensure the above is to establish a consistent mechanism to get feedback and improve. The WWW and EBI structure is really helpful and hopefully, you will really see positive changes over the course of a term.

We hope these six ideas will help you keep your students coming to class. Now let's look at how we can keep our learners central to our lessons.

Keeping people central (not the programme)

Another important aspect in retaining people is to respond to the needs of people rather than stick rigidly to a set programme. Yes, we need an objective and to keep lessons as professional as possible but we will need to demonstrate flexibility, warmth and show love and concern if we want to go deeper than simply providing English classes between the hours of 2-4 on a Thursday, for example.

It's this holistic approach to teaching English in our church that should start to differentiate what we do from other 'free' English classes that may be available.

Let's think over the next couple of pages about how we can be distinctive. Here are some ways we can do this:

1) Create a sense of belonging

This starts at the welcome. If you have ever attended a new church as a visitor, amongst other things, you are keenly aware of the welcome, the atmosphere, and perhaps whether people were generally interested in you coming, etc. You might even run through a mental checklist, comparing it to your home church or other church experiences!

So, while teaching English and reaching people for Christ are great objectives in themselves, we will do this more effectively when we are genuinely interested in each individual. Remembering the details of people's lives is important – perhaps something they had mentioned in the last class – or something you know about them.

Get your welcomers to engage with students, perhaps starting the welcome conversation next time with something they remember about what the learner had shared before:

"So, Maria, how was the interview for the job?"

or

"Last time you said your mother was poorly. Is she any better this week?"

This can really make a difference (whether in a class setting or in church services).

Being friendly, encouraging participation in lessons (and wider church if there is an appropriate event for someone who is unchurched) and creating a sense of community are all starting points that will foster a sense of belonging.

As a result, it is good to remember that English lessons at their best are part of a bigger picture for reaching internationals. They are often a stepping stone to getting to know people, developing relationships, and introducing Christ rather than an end in themselves.

In short, a well-rounded, holistic and relational approach is best. You may remember that at the beginning of this guide we included some quotes to support the biblical mandate for reaching the world for Christ. This is a given - but let us not in our eagerness to 'tell' forget to really listen and respond with grace to the people in front of us. Perhaps these quotes sum this attitude up best.

"A hungry belly has no ears" (African proverb)

"Truly, I tell you, whatever you did for one of the least of these brothers and sisters of mine, you did for me." *(Matthew 25:40)*

2) Showing cultural awareness and sensitivity

Just as important as creating a sense of belonging and inclusiveness, is making sure that we are aware of different cultures, traditions, and sensitivities in our learners.

In the West, we often are shy about talking about our culture or religion. However, for our students, religion is often a central part of their lives and cultures.

In their worldview, religion and culture might go hand-in-hand, so showing willingness to learn about both is crucial to gaining the trust of our students.

In a caring and sensitive way, find out what religious background your students are from. You might sometimes be surprised. One volunteer group was shocked to hear that their students from Afghanistan were Sikh, not Muslim. Media coverage of Afghanistan had never mentioned the other religions represented in the population.

It would be a good idea to take time with your other volunteers to research the basic tenets of your students' faiths, so you don't offend them unnecessarily. For example, Hindus believe in many deities, but Muslims and Sikhs are monotheistic, believing in only one god and might be incredibly offended if someone implies otherwise. (See **resource #15** at the end of Chapter 7 for a link to a basic overview of what other religions believe).

In addition, find out about cultural values that might be different in Western culture, but should be respected in order to win their trust. For example, many cultures are more conservative than ours in the West. Often, women are expected to dress modestly and men and women do not socialise unless they are related to each other. Muslims don't eat pork or drink alcohol, and Hindus and Sikhs are vegetarians as well as having a taboo on alcohol. While we don't have to agree with these views, respecting these differences without trying to change them allows us to build trust and relationship with the students. Building trust allows us eventually to earn a hearing for our own faith.

Also, take time in conversations after class to ask what is important to them in their religion. Do they pray? Where? At home or at a temple or mosque? What are the main holidays? What happens during those holidays? Are there special foods they eat or gifts they exchange? See how their faces light up with a chance to talk about something they know! It will help build trust, but also help their English to talk about something important to them.

Keep an eye on interpersonal dynamics so that everyone feels equally welcomed and valued in the class, and no favouritism is shown to any one nationality or religion. Christ welcomes us all as we are and we should welcome others as He welcomes us.

Many faiths welcome prayer, so showing concern for personal issues in students' lives and then offering to pray for them is often an effective bridge to both showing care and demonstrating God's care for them. Always be sure to ask the students' permission first, so they know you respect their faith.

3) Get students involved

It is great to involve your students in classes – particularly if they have had experiences that can benefit others. Here are some practical ways in which volunteers have effectively involved students in classes:

...One church realised that a class member had been successful in their asylum application and so was able to relate their experiences to the class.

...More advanced English class members have been engaged to help those who are weaker in English with form filling, translating, etc. as part of the class.

...Students are asked in advance to explain specific cultural celebrations/festivals to the class and encouraged to bring in food to share connected to the festivity.

...Ex-class members who have left class to take up work or study have themselves come back to act as volunteers.

...If a class member has achieved something they feel is significant and their English helped them do it, they have been encouraged to share it in class.

All of these can bring a greater degree of relevance to your lessons and the learning experience. It can benefit other members of the group and encourage group cohesion.

So, consider asking students for help – to set up, or put away, or help a fellow class member, or perhaps even assist in serving teas and coffees. You will need to consider how appropriate this is but part of belonging is getting involved.

Remember, most of us don't like to feel we are being 'helped' all the time. We often relish being a helper and like to be valued as part of a team and for our contributions. In summary, making sure that our classes are responsive and inclusive is an important part of the successful learning experience.

So, we have looked at the importance of keeping learners central in our lesson and ensuring our focus is on them and their learning, rather than our curriculum. We have also examined how we keep our students returning for lessons. Let's look at some of the common problems that we can face as English language teachers as we look to troubleshoot some of the most common issues.

Classroom dynamics: troubleshooting

As experienced language teachers, we know that things in the classroom often don't turn out quite like we expect them to!

There are a number of things that can go wrong, but we have outlined a few of the more obvious pitfalls below, with some tips on how to avoid them. We hope you find these helpful!

Too many different levels

It is a common problem, so if it is one you encounter, consider using model B from our two suggested class lesson approaches. An all-together session followed by group work based on level. This will allow you to differentiate for the levels, providing you have sufficient volunteers who can assist.

Not enough resources on hand

Consider an inexpensive subscription to a materials provider e.g. Handouts Online or view the resource list in the appendix.

A lot of individual English needs

If you find it difficult to address all the individual needs of the class, then once again, consider class organisation pattern B.

Beginners

Finding good materials pitched to level is certainly not easy and if you are a new teacher, this is a notoriously tricky group to teach. See the previous chapter for specific help with teaching beginners.

Inconsistent attendance

Consider charging a small amount per class and having a registration/kick off day which outlines term dates, making classes seem more professional and organised. You may consider taking contact details to follow up with those who have not been for a time. The tone in follow-up should be along the lines of 'We've missed you' rather than 'Where were you?' It is nice to be missed but not so good to feel hounded.

Dominant characters/quiet members

Consider pairing shyer members together so they are not dominated by one individual. Consider not eliciting answers from the class but instead choosing individuals to provide the answer. Try building this approach into the culture of the class, so students come to expect to answer at least one-two times per session.

Not sure if students really understand

Show and don't tell where possible, using illustrations, mimes, and video if you can to help students understand the concepts. Some nationalities will always nod to the question 'Do you understand?', so it is advisable to check with more sophisticated (but simple) questions that confirm they really do. These questions are not likely to be ones that require 'yes' or 'no' answers but will require a longer explanation and start with 'why, what, when, how', for example.

As a general tip, **don't** speak for too long – it is really hard to listen in another language for any length of time. Ensure interaction is part of the session by using pair work activities, group work activities and discussion.

Now, let's move on to look at how we can move from simply teaching English to sharing the gospel.

CHAPTER 7

SHARING THE GOSPEL

If we are going to tell of the love of Jesus, it makes sense to show it, too. We have been really heartened to hear how some churches have intentionally embraced different communities so they feel supported, loved, and welcomed.

That is an incredibly powerful combination.

So, if we are to move from English teaching to sharing the gospel, we need to think about involving the wider church we belong to.

Involving the wider church

Here, James Myles lists the ways his church, WPCA in Belfast, welcomes internationals:

"We invite them to activities the church is running e.g. mums & tots, Kids Club, music nights, a Christmas fayre, etc.

Invite them to afternoon tea & Sunday service once a month. The particular service is run by & for members of the church with learning difficulties, so the language of the service is very simple and easy to understand.

Show God's love by providing food hampers and other support for those in need.

Volunteers build up relationships with a small number of students they help in the class and take opportunities to share their faith."

Similarly, Carys Woodbridge at ELT Baptist church says:

"We have youth clubs in the church, encourage hospitality and try and encourage the congregation to get to know their neighbours, who are very likely to be from the Bangladeshi community."

Sue Wood, from Belmont church in Exeter, adds:

"One morning we have an information cafe for international women – a programme of talks, crafts, cookery and encouraging the women to tell us about their countries; e.g. origami, cooking, Nowruz – Kurdish New Year.

People in the church are part of Friends International activities, which mainly take place at our church, Belmont Chapel (free use of rooms plus financial support of worker). We run an international café, hospitality scheme, day trips, etc."

Extra services

As we can see, the wider church can play a really effective role in making internationals feel welcome and addressing some of their needs.

Indeed, English may only be part of what is on offer; a church may provide additional services such as a computer class, a crèche, charity shop, co-operative or food bank, café, job club, debt advice, etc. This extra layer of support really puts the church at the heart of the community, addressing needs holistically.

In fact, in a recent conversation, a church-based organiser said that of all the things offered through their church (English lessons, crèche, food bank etc.) it was the job club that had the most direct impact on internationals coming to faith. This may seem surprising, but she went on to explain that this was largely due to the 1-1 nature of the interaction at the job club – necessary for trying to fix people up with jobs and discovering job seekers' needs, wants and gifting.

Now, these learners needed English help in order to get to that stage but by looking after those needs holistically and dealing personally with individuals, this church-based organisation has been able to make the most impact.

Of course, it is not always possible to offer any extra support in such an organised way.

However, you could build up a list of useful contacts in order to signpost similar services in the area (such as the Citizens Advice Bureau in the

UK) or encourage other class members to share their outside agency experiences with the class, or invite speakers in to talk about the range of services and help that might be on offer.

All of these extra things could help to make the English lessons more relevant to your learners and address their specific needs more readily. This, in turn, helps your learners to see themselves as part of the church community rather than someone who is unaffiliated and simply a user of the building and resources.

Using the Bible in English classes

Teaching English provides us with a unique platform for reaching people. In class, we can share our ideas, our lives, and our motivations for living. Even when the lesson theme is not specifically Christian, we can expect that at some point a learner may ask us our views on the topic under discussion – such as attitudes to death or life, dating and relationships, family, marriage or even money.

Of course, that is an open invitation for us as Christians to share sensitively what we think about these issues.

However, should we be more intentional about bringing Jesus into our classes?

After all, helping to improve lives in this world is a wonderful thing to be able to do. But for us, as Christians, we know that this life is a mere shadow of what is to come. Real love is to share the way to eternal life through Christ.

So, if you believe that we should be more intentional about bringing the Bible into our time together with internationals, then how do we do this?

To help answer the question above, we asked a number of Christians involved in English language teaching in church about their approach. Let's see what they said. Here are real examples of what is going on currently at a few churches in the UK.

As you will see, there is no 'one-size fits all' approach but great work is being done sowing the seeds of the gospel in a variety of ways and settings.

"By providing free classes and showing unconditional love and support. This speaks of Jesus without words so that when asked for our motivation, we can give a reason for the hope we have."

"We don't usually use the Bible in our classes as many of the students are Muslims and wouldn't come if we did. However, at Christmas and Easter, we do work on the Christian stories of Christmas and Easter and sometimes good conversations

result. This is our prayer."

"We offer a general English class for the first hour. All are invited to stay on for an optional 30-minute Bible study in English at the end of the class with simplified English."

"We show films with subtitles after the classes if anyone wants to stay on – The Jesus film: "Magdalena – through her eyes") as it appeals to Middle Eastern women." (See resources).

"I don't habitually use the Bible in lessons but do use it if appropriate, e.g. in a lesson on time, I have used Ecclesiastes 3; when talking about the family, have used biblical families as examples of family relationships, etc. I don't use them evangelistically but simply as texts."

"We follow up the Easter, Christmas stories in their English classes with a relevant Bible tract in their own language they can take home."

Clearly, there is some great creative work going on to both teach English and to intentionally offer opportunities to learn more about the Christian faith.

Other ideas to introduce Jesus

We have also heard of some interesting, direct but non-threatening ways to invite learners to find out more about Jesus if they are interested.

Once, at a social event organised by Friends International, a written invitation was left on each table with international students encouraged to tick a response.

The words on the invite went something like this:

Would you be interested in finding out more about the person of Jesus and why he is important to Christians?

…I'd like a book/some reading material on Jesus
…I would like to meet 1-1
…I want to stay after class for a free group Bible class in English
…I am not interested

Your name (optional):

Thank you.

While being quite direct, this was a good way of asking whether learners wanted to find out more. Those that indicated an interest were offered extra Bible lessons after class, 1-1's or biblical tracts in their own language as appropriate.

One church has asked the non-Christians who regularly used the church centre for meetings, toddler groups, etc. if they would like the church family to pray for them. The email sent went something like this….

It is soon National Prayer Weekend (a UK-wide plan to pray for people in our communities). So, we are asking for prayer requests from groups who use the church such as toddlers, etc.

Because you are in a group which uses the church, would you like us to pray for you and/or your family? First names or no names are fine.

If you would like to email me a sentence or two (or more!) please send it through and our church family will pray for you.

The response was surprisingly positive and allowed for sensitive follow-up.

Mostly, the ideas we have introduced so far in this chapter about introducing Jesus have taken the form of invites or follow-ups to the main class. But what about using explicitly Christian material, such as a Bible story, as the basis for ESL classes? Is it wise? Will it put people off from coming?

At the two:nineteen English teaching and outreach forum in Reading, UK in 2015, a number of people spoke about their ESL work in churches. They had been right at the heart of multi-national communities, teaching English for free and doing great work for a number of years. They had a clear policy **not to use the Bible** *"...because they had never done so..."* and were trusted amongst various faith groups not to.

To suddenly begin would really put the proverbial cat amongst the pigeons and potentially lose the goodwill and trust of their communities.

In contrast, another delegate at the same forum said her church **had always used Bible-based material** in her English lessons even though their church is at the heart of a multi-faith community *"...because they had always done so...".*

So which approach is best?

It depends whether you see the focus of these classes as being to teach people English or to teach the gospel. So, it goes back to your vision, since this will largely determine class content.

The key is transparency and consistency. Learners should know what to expect. People do not like to feel manipulated and so if a group of internationals attend a class advertised simply as 'free English' lessons at a local community centre, but are met with an evangelical talk and Bible-based English materials, they may quite understandably feel duped.

There may be many good reasons for not using biblically-based materials. However, one of the main reasons for not using the Bible as a source is 'it will put people off'.

We'll briefly explore this statement in the next chapter.

Is resistance to Christianity real?

Perhaps you may wish to use the Bible as a basis for classes but are concerned about putting some people off.

However, many learners from different cultures who have made the UK their home do have a 'religious' worldview, which may underpin their outlook and behaviour. Quite often, in the appropriate context and within a non-threatening environment, they are happy to discuss what it is. This may surprise us in the increasingly secular West, where we often stay politely clear of religion – but it is true.

Islam, for example, shares many of the same prophets as Christianity. Further, many internationals will celebrate religious festivals and be keen to know the meaning of Christian ones. When considering the person of Jesus, many are respectful and Muslims are taught in the Quran to respect and revere Jesus as a prophet. His virgin birth is confirmed and some of the miracles he performed are also recorded.

A delegate at a recent conference reported such demand for their recently set up Bible-based English classes in their multi-faith locality that they now had a waiting list. In addition, many from the class had started attending church and a few had converted to Christianity. He commented that their church also engaged with the community in other ways, on the streets and they even had a market stall. Their English programme is clearly and overtly a Christian outreach and far from being off-putting, many from the multi-faith community around them have embraced it.

However, it is also true that while there may be some faith commonalities, many internationals may have a distinctly negative view of Christianity. Indeed, many see Christianity as a Western faith that is generally lived out in a rather weak and lacklustre way. Some cultures may view Western society as morally corrupt and see this 'broken society' as inextricably linked to a Christianity.

Having said that, this negative attitude towards Western culture does not normally carry over to opinions about Jesus himself.

It makes sense, therefore, to talk less about *denominations* and *religion* and talk more about Jesus; his life, his teachings, and his death on the cross. The significance of this for everyone in the world might be of more interest to our learners than we would think.

We are not denying that in some places there is real resistance to Christianity. Some will see it as a complete turn off from lessons, as we have seen above. But we shouldn't take that to mean there is resistance across the board.

We suggest you prayerfully consider whether it is appropriate where you are, in your locality, to make lessons biblically-based. Also, to pray for openings to share the love of Jesus, be that in class, after class, 1-1 or as a follow-on Bible study. Pray for Jesus to open the hearts of your learners so that however and whenever the gospel is shared, they will be receptive and that many will come to know Him as their personal saviour.

Material for Bible-based classes

When talking about our faith in the classroom, where should we start? Certainly, the life of Jesus is a good place to begin. Similarly, so are stories from the Old Testament with prophets such as Moses and Abraham. If you have Muslim students, these figures will be familiar. These are often more accessible than a Psalm or a New Testament letter as a first step into the Bible.

Additionally, stories (with a beginning, middle and end) are universally attractive and conceptually easier for language students to grasp. One of the resources at the end of this chapter links to Bible-based PDF lessons from Adam and Eve to the resurrection. See #2 **From Beginning to End**. You can also summarise the story, discuss the underlying meaning, etc.

What follows are three sample lessons that incorporate a Bible story, which we have built some English lessons around.

For the first example, we have chosen a fairly straightforward Bible story from the Old Testament (**God's call to Abram**) and then given some ideas for how we could use it in an English class. We suggest this would be appropriate for a lower level group, although not beginners, as the language level is too high for this level.

Then, for the second example, we have selected a lesson about **grace**, which can be a challenging concept for learners to grasp. However, we have selected a Bible reading and then some additional activities around it so you can work through the idea in a structured way with a class. This would probably be most appropriate for a group of an intermediate level or higher.

Then finally, a third lesson based on **the prodigal son**. This is quite visual and is customisable for different levels.

Let's look at the three further lesson ideas, one by one, starting with **God's call of Abram.**

Lesson idea 9

God calls Abram (based on Genesis 12:1-3)

Have the story printed out, but with some words missing. Get the students to guess what the words might be before you read the story aloud. When you read aloud, the students complete the gaps with the words they hear.

Now God said to Abram, "_____ your country, your relatives, and your father's _____. _____ to the land I will show you. Then I will _____ you into a great nation, and I will

_____ you. Your name _____ _____ great.

I will _____ those who _____ you. I will _____ those who _____ you. And all the people on earth will be blessed _____ you."

Here is the completed version:

Now God said to Abram, "<u>Leave</u> your country, your relatives, and your father's <u>house</u>. <u>Go</u> to the land I will show you. Then I will <u>make</u> you into a great nation, and I will <u>bless</u> you. Your name <u>will</u> <u>be</u> great.

I will <u>bless</u> those who <u>bless</u> you. I will <u>curse</u> those who <u>curse</u> you. And all the people on earth will be blessed <u>through</u> you."

The idea of this exercise is to get students used to listening and recognising words that are not written down and seeing how they fit into the sentence.

Next, cut the narrative into strips and have the students arrange the strips in order so they tell the story. Then have them read the complete story afterwards – does it make sense in the order that they have arranged it?

Then ask some basic questions about the text to check understanding, such as:

1. What did God tell Abram to do?

2. What three things did God promise for Abram and his family?

3. How did Abram show that he believed God and trusted Him?

Students could work in pairs or small groups for this activity, find the answers and then prepare responses in English.

To conclude, have students tell the story in their own words. This helps fluency and you can practise accuracy with the past tenses.

Next, explain:

Abraham (Abram) is an important figure in the Bible. Abraham said yes to God. God kept His promise. Abraham had a son, who had a son, who had a son and so on. Christians believe that Jesus is Abraham's descendant.

(Read Matthew 1:1 and maybe draw an outline of a family tree so students get the idea.) Christians believe that God kept His promises to Abraham by giving us Jesus.

But, Jesus also said he was more than a relation of Abraham.

(Hand out the following and have students complete on their own. Let them think through the implication and invite feedback.)

Jesus told the people that:

Abraham saw the day He (Jesus) would come and was happy. (John 8:56)

and

The fact is, before Abraham was born, I AM (John 8: 58)

Abraham was born about 2000 years before Jesus. How can Jesus have seen Abraham?

I Am is the name God called himself in the Old Testament. What is Jesus saying about himself?

For similar Bible reading lessons, see resource #2 **From Beginning to End** on the further resources page at the end of this chapter. These are available free via PDF online.

Lesson idea 10

If you have more advanced learners, perhaps consider introducing more challenging concepts of biblical grace/forgiveness with short modern-day equivalents so you can show the concepts rather than tell.

The following lesson idea is best given either before or after a lesson on the resurrection - as an introduction or consolidation of the story.

Guilty or Innocent?

Start by ensuring your students understand the meaning of these words:

trial, jury, court, judge, guilty, innocent, jail, to be punished.

You could have students match the word to the explanations, for example. You could draw a courtroom on the board/find a picture of one and label the judge, jury, and a jail, etc.

Tell the class you are in the jury watching a trial. A man, let's call him Robert, has fought with his family, lived away from them, lived a bad life, and stolen something and goes to court. His crimes are read out. The court says Robert is guilty. The judge says he will be sent to jail.

Suddenly, Robert's father stands up and says he will take the punishment for the crimes. You watch as Robert goes free. The innocent man, Robert's father, is punished and sent to jail.

Ask questions like:

1. Did the father deserve to go to prison? (No)

2. Did the son deserve to go free? (No)

3. Why might the father do this? (He loves the son.)

4. What might the son think about the father now? (He can say sorry, be grateful or he may choose to ignore his father still and continue his bad life.)

Then say:

"Christians believe we are all like Robert – we don't

obey God and we don't live lives that please God. If God is the judge, we are all guilty because of how we think, speak and live. God calls ignoring Him and living our way sin. Sin is disgusting to a holy, perfect God. We deserve to be punished by God for this disgusting sin.

But God so loves us, He sent His son, Jesus. Jesus is perfect and holy, too, and did nothing wrong. Like the father in the story, he took our punishment. Jesus died on a cross taking our punishment.

The Bible says that when we trust what Jesus has done for us, we are free from punishment. When we trust what Jesus has done for us, we are not separated from God by sin. We are acceptable to God – now and forever.

But, we can choose to accept that Jesus-gift or not. Where in the Bible does it say that? In several places, but here it is in just one verse..." (give the verse out):

"God so loved the world that he gave his one and only Son, that whoever believes in him shall not die but have eternal life." (John 3: 16) NIV

Next, students work in pairs (suggested responses are in brackets). According to the Bible verse:

1) Why did God send his son, Jesus to die for us? (Because He loved us.)

2) What does eternal life mean? (Now and after death…in heaven.)

3) How does the Bible say we can be right with God now and enjoy life with Him now and forever? (By trusting in Jesus. By saying 'Yes' to Jesus. We can take this further and say: by understanding sin means we cannot be right with God. There is nothing we can do. Only Jesus can make us right with God).

Now, give students 10 minutes on their own to write any questions they have/comments anonymously. Collect them in. Write one on the board, invite the class to correct any English, then answer/address the comment. Move on to the next question and so on.

For a final plan, let's look at the story of the prodigal son, from Luke Ch. 15.

Lesson idea 11

Welcome home?

Start: if possible, tie a line of string from one end of the classroom to the other and introduce it to the class as a washing line. Read the following:

A son has lived a bad life away from his parents. He now has no money and no friends and is sad. He writes home to say sorry to his parents and asks to come home. He says he wants to return but is not sure if his parents will welcome him. So, he asks his parents to put a white towel on the washing line in the back garden if he is welcome. (Peg a white towel on the line.)

 If he is not welcome, they are not to put any towel out. (Take the white towel off.)

He will see this towel before he gets to their street. Then, he will know if he is welcome at his parents' house.

Check students understand. Peg the white towel up. Ask:

Is the son welcome?

Take it off. Ask again:

If the son sees this, no towel, is he welcome home?

Continue with the story:

The day arrives. The young man arrives back to his hometown by train. Walking along the street next to his parents' street, he suddenly stops. He is too worried to turn the corner to look at the washing line. So, he asks someone if he will look around the corner to see if there is a white towel on the washing line in his parents' garden. The man looks and then tells the young man to look. The son sees there is white towels and sheets everywhere, over the trees, fences, gardens, clothesline –

everywhere is covered.

At this point, spread white sheets, pillow cases and paper over the front of the classroom.

Students discuss in pairs:

1. Why was the son worried? (He lived a bad life, he didn't deserve to come home/ashamed.)

2. How much did the parents want to forgive and welcome their son? (Lots!)

3. Did the boy deserve this welcome and love? (No)

Discuss the answers as a class afterwards to ensure everyone understands.

Follow-up 1:

Students write a *"Can I come home?"* letter to the parents, pretending to be the son, or students write and role-play the dialogue of the parent/son first conversation after being welcomed back.

Say:

Jesus used a similar story to tell us how much we are loved, forgiven and welcomed by our father God when we say sorry to Him.

The story tells us we don't deserve God's love and forgiveness but when we say sorry He forgives us and welcomes us like these parents did when their son came home.

Follow-up 2:

This is how Jesus explained the way the father welcomed the son who was sorry and returned home. Give this version out to each student. It is based on the EasyEnglish version of the Bible (see resources) but simplified further. Start in class, students can complete at home.

Based on Luke 15: 20-24

The son returned to his father. When his father saw him coming he ran to him and put his arms around him and kissed him. 'I am sorry, Father", said the son. 'I have done bad things against God and against you. So you must not call me your son.' But the father told the servants 'Give my son the most beautiful coat that we have. Put a ring on one of his fingers. Put shoes on his feet. Get the young, fat cow that we keep to eat on a special day. Kill it - we shall eat a big meal and be happy together. I thought my son was dead. But now he has returned to me alive. I thought that he had left me forever. But now he has come home.' Then they began to be happy together.

Get everyone to read the above aloud together.

Ask:

1. Was the son in the story sorry?

2. How did the father show the son he was

welcome?

3. Why did the father welcome the son home?

4. The father in the story is supposed to be God. What is Jesus saying about the character of God?

5. The son in the story is supposed to be us. What does Jesus say about what we have to do to be welcomed/accepted by God?

Homework:

Highlight the following words from the story. Use the words in the box to make complete sentences based on the story (don't look back at the complete story).

Now, use linking words like *and then, next,* etc. between the sentences you have created to make a fluent story without looking at the original.

The son returned
When his father saw
Kissed
I am sorry, Father.
Coat
Ring
Shoes
Kill
Eat
I thought my son was dead but…
I thought he had left me but….
Happy

Simplifying the Bible message?

What you will have noticed in the above examples is that the lessons introduce and deal with biblical principles in quite a simple way.

There is far more to the prodigal son story, for example, but for non-native speakers, we do have to make a choice about the focus of the story and the language we use in the explanation. Some of this will be dependent on the level or ability of your learners.

There is a real tension in simplifying the message yet keeping to biblical truth. We may fear that we are somehow 'dumbing down' or missing essential biblical points. This is something Ferris Lindsay, an experienced teacher in an East London church, knows all too well.

Here is how Ferris introduced the concept of **sacrifice** to his ELT class – and how he felt about his explanations afterwards:

*"Today, we were to study Jesus arranging a private Passover Meal with his disciples. Before we read it, we introduced the word **sacrifice**.*

Easy enough to get this over to the Muslims in class (they make a sacrifice at Eid-al-Adha). The idea of giving something up is universal (I should think).

But animal sacrifice? How to explain this? Difficulty

number one: I saw what I thought was a flinch on the faces of our two Hindu learners. It reminded me that the idea of killing any animal is an abomination to Hindus (I think).

And here we have God telling his people to kill a lamb as a sacrifice for their wrong. Oh dear. Change of tack time. I needed to acknowledge the ugliness of animal sacrifice (and it is ugly!). I said:

The lamb had never lied, or stolen or done anything to deserve death. It really was sad and terrible. But there was something more ugly than that.

Next up, I wanted to press home the idea that our sin made us ugly and unacceptable to God - this really mattered. That's why I spoke of myself.

I said that; my wrongdoing and wrong thinking makes me disgusting to God.

*They all got the word **disgusting**. But isn't that a bit strong? I continued:*

Well, we might be used to our wrongdoing: our greed, laziness, jealousies, anger, selfishness etc. We just accept them (along with the good we do) as part of being human. But God doesn't.

There was some recognition on several faces.

*That's where sacrifice comes in. It is there as a **payment,** not to pay for our wrong but to temporarily turn aside the anger of God. He is* *willing to take us at our word that we are sorry and to eventually provide a payment himself.*

I said:

See this disgusting person (me). Jesus said that he would take my place and the punishment due to me.

I was encouraged that after class, one of the Tamil learners said,

"It was good that you blamed yourself".

There were times when I felt the embarrassment that comes from simplifying truth. I know that my discourse would be embarrassing to a native English speaker.

But then I was reminded that I am not speaking to native English speakers so I shouldn't judge my language as though I was. No. You speak to who is in front of you. And you make sure they can understand you.

God give me the ability to be clear and understandable to those in front of me and to leave the   rest   to   you."

We can recommend some simplified biblical texts for you:

First, there is an excellent version of **Christianity Explored for internationals,** published by the UK

Christian student befriending organisation, Friends International. **The Visa Course** (see resource #8 on further resources at the end of this chapter) aims to open the Bible using simplified English and in a culturally sensitive way. There is an inexpensive booklet for both leader and student.

You may choose not to use this material as a course but it is worth it for some suitable Bible passages in easy English, great tips on cultural sensitivity and because it provides a wealth of lead-in and follow-up discussion questions around the life of Jesus.

The **Good book blog** has also published some great and visual gospel overviews online which can be simplified further for learners of English. (See resource #13 at the end of this chapter.)

The **EasyEnglish Bible** with commentaries, studies, and a book overview vocabulary is also available online. See resource #5 at the end of this chapter.

Not every class with a Christian theme has to be based on a biblical text. Most learners will be interested in why we celebrate certain festivals and the origins of these festivals. Many have Christian origins and so, in addition to Easter and Christmas, there are St. Patrick's Day, Pancake Day, or the run-up to Easter during Lent, for example. Here is just one example of a Christian festival lesson:

http://www.eslholidaylessons.com/02/pancake_day.html

It is also possible to look at the basis of some of our laws in the UK and share the Christian perspective on these and on views of what we consider right or wrong. Issues of life after death, how we look at money, debt, education, conservation, etc. are all topics that can be explored sensitively. **Spotlight radio** produces broadcasts which are not overtly Christian but have a positive and Christian-based worldview and can be useful to stimulate discussions. See resource #9 under Sharing the Gospel resources.

Tip: Whether we decide to use Bible-based materials or not, it may be wise to discuss your approach with your volunteers and helpers. For example, you may want to chat through the following together:

...How might we explain the gospel message simply?
...Do we need to practise this so we are indeed ready to give a reason for the hope that we have, simply, and in a way that can be clearly understood?

Here's a simple overview for leaders and volunteers, like a Q&A:

http://www.christianwitnessingtools.com/core-message.html

It is important that we all come from the same direction when we have the opportunity to share the gospel; the opportunity might come when you are least expecting it! So do be prepared for when your student asks you about your faith. It might just be the most important conversation you have this week/month/year!

Now, before we finish, here are a few final tips on teaching English using the Bible.

Some final tips on teaching English using the Bible

Tip: *Do try to include some application questions where possible, so that the biblical text is not just a background to English but is made relevant to their lives now.*

These might be something as simple as:

...Does Jesus' attitude surprise you? How? ...If what Jesus says is true – how should we respond?

If this does not seem appropriate or you are concerned that it might put individuals 'on the spot' in class, you could give them a question or two to think through at home.

Tip: *If you can, make yourself available after class for a few minutes, inviting anyone who wants to stay on and ask questions about English or the content. You might find some students have good, searching questions but feel inhibited about voicing these in front of others.*

Tip: *Do be respectful of other faiths and ensure your language is not inflammatory or likely to cause people to become offended. Remember that we are not here to convert people (only God can do that) but simply to point people to Jesus and what he has done for us through His death and resurrection.*

Tip: *Don't assume that your understanding of who God or Jesus is –or what heaven is– is the same as your learners, even if they are using the same words. Most people have different starting points, influenced by their background, culture and education. For example, God in Islam is not knowable or relatable. While Hindus believe in an afterlife, they also believe there are many roads to it.*

Further resources for Sharing the Gospel

Bible/bible based resources for class use:

1. English in Action
Bible picture stories with key vocabulary: ideal for lower level learners. Available via Amazon although it may be wise to invest additionally in the teacher's book to get the best out of the material. Not cheap but covers a whole approach to teaching. Student book:
http://amzn.to/2symyxk

2. From Beginning to End
10 Bible-based reading lessons free via PDF with ESL tasks and discussion questions; from Adam and Eve to the resurrection with a final summary lesson:
http://www.eslbible.org/

3. SELB
Society for English learning through biblical literature. Try a sample from the ACE course here before buying: http://selbl.frasertec.com/index.asp plus you can register for free lesson plans for English learning through the bible here: http://bit.ly/1PE76ol

4. NIRV (New International Readers Version)
Simplified English Bible:
http://www.biblestudytools.com/nirv/

5. EasyEnglish
Bible, book overviews, commentaries using a 1200-word vocabulary: level A, or 2800 words level B:
http://www.easyenglish.info/

6. Literacy and Evangelism International
A training and publication organisation based in the USA aiming to equip Christians to help with literacy through the Bible. Various handbooks to buy: http://store.literacyevangelism.org/

7. The Jesus film: Magdalena – through her eyes
http://www.magdalenatoday.com/ shows Jesus through a woman's eyes. There are more Christian resources around women on the site. Part of a larger project 'The Jesus Film' http://jesusfilm.org/ and available to watch in different languages.

8. The Visa course
Friends International adapted Christianity Explored course for internationals. Student and teacher book available cheaply:
http://friendsinternational.uk/resources/books-to-buy/visa-course-student-notes

9. Spotlight
Audio broadcast. 'Light' Christian theme. Ideal for improving listening skills and for further discussion. Skype English clubs have been set up around them:
http://www.spotlightenglish.com/about

10. TalkEnglish
Brings learners and Christians together so learners can practise English through the Bible. To access materials, you will need to register as an instructor. Looks a little complex to get started? http://bit.ly/1LB3Zlu

11. The prodigal son
Modern story for advanced learners on the **Faithpal** blog:
http://thefaithpal.blogspot.co.uk/2010/03/prodigal-son-and-forgiving-father.html

12. ESL holiday lessons
This is on Pancake day. Links to other celebrations can be found but are less well linked to Christian foundations:
http://www.eslholidaylessons.com/02/pancake_day.html

13. Good Book Blog Gospel illustrations. Intended for children, but very visual and can be adapted for language learners:
http://www.thegoodbook.co.uk/blog/?qb=ultimate+gospel+illustrations

14. Christianity Explored Universal: a simplified international version of the Christianity Explored course for internationals.
An inexpensive workbook based on the Gospel of Mark:
https://www.thegoodbook.co.uk/christianity-explored-universal-handbook

15. What do different faiths believe: A short, overview finishing with why Christianity is different:
http://www.everystudent.com/features/connecting.html

CHAPTER 8

THE NEXT STEP TO GETTING STARTED

We hope that in reading this you will feel challenged and inspired to get involved in some way. Yes, there are things to consider in setting up or contributing to a teaching English in church programme - but despite challenges of time and resources, most volunteers were overwhelmingly positive about the experience. When we asked them to impart their advice to you about getting started, here's what they said:

"When we thought about setting it up, we imagined committees, meetings, and a long process. Eventually, we thought: we could talk about this all year; let's just do it."

"...have a go! Talk first to people already doing it to get some practical advice, but there are always people around who are keen to improve their English so it's a great opportunity to reach out to the local community."

"...source another church that is already running classes to get a feel for how they look and what they do before committing time and people to a new one. Offer to volunteer for a while. The

experience gained will be invaluable."

In fact, the sentiments expressed are best summed up by Sue Wood of Belmont church, Exeter:

"Go for it, lots of fun."

Over to you - please share your experiences

We like to think of this as a living, breathing guide and want to keep it as up-to-date as possible. We'd love to hear from you if you are keen to:

…share 'best practice'
…add something you think is missing
…provide some advice, top tips or link to useful resources you've found
…report a broken link

In the first instance, please email us at Christian TEFL:
info@christiantefl.org.

We have really enjoyed putting together this guide and we hope you find it of help and benefit as you seek to serve Him through teaching English, wherever you are in the world. God bless.

CHAPTER 9

FURTHER RESOURCES SUMMARY

Resources are listed by the chapter in which they appear.

Chapter 3 – Getting Started

Teacher training courses/networking/support/forums:

1. Christian TEFL
Accredited online TEFL training courses for Christians:
Courses from 70-250 hours, plus CPD for already trained teachers:
www.christiantefl.org

2. Global English TESOL
Accredited online TESOL courses and short weekend courses. Sister organisation to Christian TEFL, over 20 years' experience in distance-based TEFL training:
www.global-english.com

3. Friends International's Teaching English Network Facebook group
https://www.facebook.com/groups/TENetwork/

4. Two:nineteen
English teaching and outreach forum:

http://www.englishandoutreach.com/

5. ODILS, Plymouth
General English classes; focus on asylum seekers.
Trinity TESOL courses in a Christian environment:
http://www.odils.com/index.php/en/

6. Bridges Language schools
Model documents, advice and support for those
starting language schools in churches:
Courses from 70-250 hours, plus CPD for already
trained teachers:
http://www.twonineteen.org.uk/how-can-we-help/bridges/

7. Glasgow asylum seeker support project - PDF
A little dated, but easy to read and provides an
interesting overview and case studies:
http://bit.ly/1kmwanO

Chapter 4 – Creating lessons

General English learning resources ready to print or buy:

1. 50 conversation classes
See a free 35-page sample online here:
http://bit.ly/1M5f4Hk
but an inexpensive hard copy is also available on
Amazon.

2. ESOL lesson plans
Free online - just select the level and skill you want to practise at the Skills Workshop site:
http://www.skillsworkshop.org/esol

3. iteslj
Hundreds of free ready-to-use discussion topics and questions organised by theme at the iteslj site:
http://iteslj.org/questions/

4. Breaking News English
Online, free news items arranged by level. You can listen, read and do the exercises:
http://www.breakingnewsenglish.com/

5. OnestopEnglish
Online, free monthly news items arranged by level with useful post-reading exercises and answer key:
http://bit.ly/1m2L0ze

6. ESOL Activities
Photocopiable lessons. Entry level 1 Book with audio CD. Look inside on the Amazon site. Also available - level 2 & 3:
http://amzn.to/1ZUcY1a

7. Handouts Online
Access hundreds of ready to use plans for a very cheap yearly subscription:
http://handoutsonline.com/

8. English Grammar in Use
Fantastic book resource for the teacher: simple grammar explanations, exercises and answer key. Such a popular title, you should easily be able to order second-hand:
http://amzn.to/1XhLDDP

9. Your English Source
ESOL photocopiables, task sheets and teacher notes for field trips like 'at the grocery store' or 'cooking.' Try 3 free and download 40 such lessons for between $5 and $15.
http://yourenglishsource.com/activity-based/

10. iSLCollective
Free ESL printables made by teachers from iSLCollective. You'll need to sign-up as a member, then download for free:
https://en.islcollective.com/resources/printables

Chapter 5 – Teaching beginners

Websites/materials for teaching those with little or no English:

1. Springinstitute.org
PDFs for teaching asylum seekers and refugees. E.g.: includes working with preliterate and non-literate learners:
https://www.springinstitute.org/esl-resources/

2. **iteslj** 1-page overview on approaches at **iteslj.org**:
http://iteslj.org/Techniques/Andrews-Beginners.html

3. **OnestopEnglish**
Step-by-step 10 lessons for absolute beginners free online with teaching notes:
http://www.onestopenglish.com/esol/absolute-beginners/unit-2/
Each plan is split into 2: for learners with and without knowledge of the Roman script.

4. **Excellence Gateway**
Step-by-step curriculum for ESOL entry level 1, 2 and 3 (elementary, pre-intermediate and intermediate levels learners), some excellent beginner material: colourful and vivid but you have to click on a link to each individual unit, which is rather cumbersome:
http://esol.excellencegateway.org.uk/vocabulary/EGaudience/learning-materials

5. **Minnesota Literacy Council**
Simple ESL lessons for everyday activities. Free and online: at work, calling in sick to a child's school, at the clinic. Each lesson starts with pictures/photos to outline the concept. The story or dialogue follows with questions underneath. Useful ideas at the start of the document and there is a sample plan at the end:
http://mnliteracy.org/sites/default/files/beginning_esl_story_bank.pdf

6. **Skills workshop** - printable and ready-to-use lessons for ESOL classes. At the drop-down, select (E1 which is entry level, meaning low 'elementary' level – above beginner) and at the 'subject area' drop-down, select what you want to practise. Some good lesson ideas with accompanying worksheets: http://bit.ly/1W3v0id

7. Skills Workshop - 100 most frequent words in alphabetical order:
http://www.skillsworkshop.org/resources/100-keywords-alphabetical-order

8. ESL flashcards
Free, downloadable and printable flashcards:
http://www.eslflashcards.com/

9. Pictures of English Tenses Elementary
View and download this book online:
http://bit.ly/1W2yz2G

Chapter 7 – Sharing the Gospel

Bible/bible based resources for class use:

1. English in Action
Bible picture stories with key vocabulary: ideal for lower level learners. Available via Amazon although it may be wise to invest additionally in the teacher's book to get the best out of the material. Not cheap but covers a whole approach to teaching. Student book:
http://amzn.to/2symyxk

2. From Beginning to End
10 Bible-based reading lessons free via PDF with ESL tasks and discussion questions; from Adam and Eve to the resurrection with a final summary lesson:
http://www.eslbible.org/

3. SELB

Society for English learning through biblical literature. Try a sample from the ACE course here before buying: http://selbl.frasertec.com/index.asp plus you can register for free lesson plans for English learning through the bible here: http://bit.ly/1PE76ol

4. NIRV (New International Readers Version)

Simplified English Bible: http://www.biblestudytools.com/nirv/

5. EasyEnglish

Bible, book overviews, commentaries using a 1200-word vocabulary: level A, or 2800 words level B: http://www.easyenglish.info/

6. Literacy and Evangelism International

A training and publication organisation based in the USA aiming to equip Christians to help with literacy through the Bible. Various handbooks to buy: http://store.literacyevangelism.org/

7. The Jesus film: Magdalena – through her eyes

http://www.magdalenatoday.com/ shows Jesus through a woman's eyes. There are more Christian resources around women on the site. Part of a larger project 'The Jesus Film' http://jesusfilm.org/ and available to watch in different languages.

8. The Visa course
Friends International adapted Christianity Explored course for internationals. Student and teacher book available cheaply:
http://friendsinternational.uk/resources/books-to-buy/visa-course-student-notes

9. Spotlight
Audio broadcast. 'Light' Christian theme. Ideal for improving listening skills and for further discussion. Skype English clubs have been set up around them:
http://www.spotlightenglish.com/about

10. TalkEnglish
Brings learners and Christians together so learners can practise English through the Bible. To access materials, you will need to register as an instructor. Looks a little complex to get started?
http://bit.ly/1LB3Zlu

11. The prodigal son
Modern story for advanced learners on the **Faithpal** blog:
http://thefaithpal.blogspot.co.uk/2010/03/prodigal-son-and-forgiving-father.html

12. ESL holiday lessons
This is on Pancake day. Links to other celebrations can be found but are less well linked to Christian foundations:
http://www.eslholidaylessons.com/02/pancake_day.html

13. **Good Book Blog** Gospel illustrations. Intended for children, but very visual and can be adapted for language learners:
http://www.thegoodbook.co.uk/blog/?qb=ultimate+gospel+illustrations

14. **Christianity Explored Universal:** a simplified international version of the Christianity Explored course for internationals.
An inexpensive workbook based on the Gospel of Mark: https://www.thegoodbook.co.uk/christianity-explored-universal-handbook

15. **What do different faiths believe:** A short, easy-to-read overview finishing in why Christianity is different:
http://www.everystudent.com/features/connecting.html

We know that links can go out of date quite quickly. However, if you do find a broken link, please contact us at the email address below. We will endeavour to maintain an accurate and updated list of resources on our website at:

www.christiantefl.org.

If you can help us add to our list, please contact us at info@christiantefl.org.

ABOUT THE AUTHOR

William Bradridge has been in English language teaching since 1990, when he starting his teaching career in Mexico City. He gained his Trinity Dip. TESOL at St George International School in London in 1995 and managed language schools in both the UK and Portugal. In 1997 he helped to set up Global English TESOL, now one of the UK's foremost accredited online TESOL course providers, and has overseen the training of thousands of new EFL teachers. Currently he spends most of his time developing EFL course materials and helping train new EFL teachers through Christian TEFL, the Christian outreach arm of Global English.

He is married to Louisa and they have two grown up daughters. He enjoys travelling and walking with the family dog, Star, around the Devon countryside and his hometown of Exeter, UK.

71731057R00085